Forty Days with the Messiah

Forty Days with the
MESSIAH

Day-by-day reflections on the words of Handel's oratorio

David Winter

The Bible Reading Fellowship
OPENING THE BIBLE

Text copyright © David Winter 1996

The author asserts the moral right to be
identified as the author of this work.

Published by
The Bible Reading Fellowship
Peter's Way, Sandy Lane West
Oxford OX4 5HG
ISBN 0 7459 3299 1
Albatross Books Pty Ltd
PO Box 320, Sutherland
NSW 2232, Australia
ISBN 0 7324 1551 9

First edition 1996
10 9 8 7 6 5 4 3 2 1 0

Acknowledgments
Unless otherwise stated, scripture quotations
referring to the words of Handel's *Messiah*
are taken from the Authorized Version of the
Bible (AV). Extracts from the Authorized
Version of the Bible (The King James Bible),
the rights in which are vested in the Crown,
are reproduced by permission of the Crown's
patentee, Cambridge University Press.

Unless otherwise stated, other scripture
quotations are taken from the New Revised
Standard Version of the Bible copyright ©
1989 by the Division of Christian Education
of the National Council of the Churches of
Christ in the USA.

Extracts denoted (BCP) are from the *Book of
Common Prayer*. Extracts from the *Book of
Common Prayer* of 1662, the rights in which
are invested in the Crown in perpetuity within the United Kingdom, are reproduced by
permission of the Crown's patentee,
Cambridge University Press.

A catalogue record for this book is
available from the British Library

Printed and bound in Great Britain
by Cox and Wyman Limited, Reading

CONTENTS

FOREWORD

Messiah was frequently revised by Handel, sometimes for artistic purposes, but more frequently to adapt to changed conditions of performance. Even in this century there have been four different editions of the work based on original sources. Accounts suggest that Handel's choir comprised four or six trebles and thirteen men. However, the centenary of his death was celebrated in Westminster Abbey with a huge choir, and since then performances in the Royal Albert Hall and other such venues throughout the country have used forces as large as 500 plus. Mozart adapted the work in 1789 for increased resources and this version was the basis of the score generally used until the present century.

In more recent times, more 'authentic' performances have become popular, using baroque instruments and fewer voices. This in turn prompted quicker tempi and a clearer 'view' of the forward thrust of the drama and the overall tonal structure of the work. Massed performances have their place and can have an impressive impact, but generally the greater the number of performers, the slower the tempi, making *Messiah* sound like a nineteenth-century work. Often a small-scale intimate performance will bring the listener closer to the heart of the work.

No recording can replace the experience of a live and complete performance. However, the cassette which complements this book includes some of the more intimate movements of the work, recorded by just four members of St Margaret's Choir and accompanied by five strings and a chamber organ.

Simon Over
Director of Music, St Margaret's Church, Westminster Abbey
July 1996

INTRODUCTION

*M*essiah is a work on the grand scale. It sets out to do nothing less than tell the story of the redemption of the human race. It is panoramic, beginning with the voice of God promising salvation and ending with the chorus of angels celebrating its completion. While it tells the story of Jesus—though scarcely at all in the language of the Gospel narratives—it is much more than that. It is the story of the Messiah. In other words, it is a declaration of the purposes of God in history.

The work is, of course, very popular and highly familiar to many people. But the problem with familiarity is that it can breed, if not contempt, then at least carelessness. We take familiar words for granted, no matter how grand and awesome they are. So for many of us *Messiah* is about good tunes, rousing choruses and haunting solos, rather than the infinite purposes of God. This book is an attempt to redress the balance. In this case, the words do matter!

For example, people often speak of 'Jesus Christ', rather as though 'Jesus' was his given name (which it was) and 'Christ' his surname (which it wasn't). To his family he was 'Jesus', one of the most common Jewish male names at the time. It's a variant of 'Joshua', and means 'saviour', 'deliverer'. To his disciples and to the crowds in Galilee and Jerusalem he was 'Rabbi', 'Teacher'. As his authority grew, many began to call him *Kyrios*, 'Lord'—one who should be respected and honoured.

But it was only with painful slowness, if we are to believe the Gospel records, that even his closest followers came to recognize that he was 'the Christ'—'the Messiah'. Both titles mean 'Anointed One', the first in Greek, the second in Hebrew. For the Twelve, it would seem that the moment of recognition was somewhere on the road to Caesarea Philippi, when Jesus asked them who they would say that he was. Peter spoke for them all: 'The Christ [Messiah] of God', he replied (Luke 9:20). It was a defining moment, both for them and for Jesus. From then on his ministry shifted its emphasis. Now there were fewer miracles, less time spent teaching the crowds. Instead, he concentrated on the little group of disciples, setting out for them the path that lay ahead of him: rejection, death, resurrection.

They found it hard to comprehend. Although such a messiah

was described in the writings of Isaiah, it was not an image that they found either familiar or appealing. They were looking for a king in the Davidic mould, a conqueror and liberator, not a Suffering Servant who would die for the people. They failed fully to comprehend the very scriptures which they knew so well.

Handel, and his librettist, Charles Jennens, came to the vast story of our redemption with seventeen centuries of Christian history behind them. For them, the story was neither unfamiliar nor unappealing. Yet as they began to unfold the scriptures, especially the writings of the great Hebrew prophets, I think they found its dimensions quite overwhelming. For what they had set themselves to do was to stretch out before their audiences the vast story of God and the human race. Only the words of scripture itself, and only truly inspired music, could even begin to do justice to a theme of such magnificence.

That is what *Messiah* offers us—the story of God's purpose in sending his 'Anointed One' to the rescue of a lost and enslaved people. It is the story of our sin, and God's grace. It is the story of the triumph of love over all the powers of evil.

Author's note

This book can be read in sections, or as daily reflections. Obviously it will be most effective if the reading can be accompanied by the music, either before or after reading. To help with this, a cassette of extracts from *Messiah* has been produced, specifically for use with this book. The performance, by members of the choir of St Margaret's, Westminster, is designed to aid reflection on the words and themes of the work. The text of *Messiah* is a finely constructed piece of biblical interpretation, bringing together prophecy, narrative, worship and praise to create an integrated picture of the whole scheme of redemption. I hope you enjoy giving it the attention it deserves!

This book is based on the libretto of *Messiah*, which is drawn, and in some cases slightly adapted, from the Authorized Version of the Bible or the Psalter of the Book of Common Prayer. Each chapter sets out the relevant part of the libretto.

After the biblical quotations, in each chapter there is a paragraph in bold type. This is an introductory thought or 'way in' to the theme of the reflection, summing up the main point, and acting as a 'hook' on which to 'hang' your understanding of the chapter.

THE COMING MESSIAH: PROMISE AND WARNING

It's early morning, and the city is just beginning business. The market traders are laying out their wares—cloths, wool, olive oil, sweet spices, oranges, lemons and grapes. The sun is casting sharp shadows in the narrow streets. There is noise—voices, cart-wheels, the harsh shriek of camels. All seems normal enough, and yet over the city of Jerusalem there is palpable fear. The Babylonians, who have already conquered the northern province of Israel, are now swarming over the surrounding countryside of Judah. Now and then, as you look from the walls towards the distant hills, you can catch the glint of sun on a helmet or a chariot. Slowly, irresistibly it seems, they are moving in on their prey...

Eventually, it happened. The defenders of the city were powerless. Just as the great prophet Isaiah had foretold a century earlier, the temple was ransacked and thousands of able-bodied men and women were taken away into captivity in Babylon. For those left behind things were not much better. The Babylonians ruled the land, set the laws, plundered the harvest. If this was, as the prophet had said, God's judgment on their past sin and disobedience, then a very heavy price was being exacted. Not for the first time, the people of Israel and Judah wondered whether being a 'chosen' people was such a privilege after all.

And where was the 'messiah'? Where was the anointed servant of God who would restore the long-lost glory of Israel and once again rule from the throne of David? How long must his downtrodden people wait before the Lord heard their cries and came to their aid?

That, in brief, is the 'story' at the point where Handel's *Messiah* begins. The prophet Isaiah had warned the kings and the people of Judah of inevitable disaster if they persisted in their idolatry and religious compromise. Chapter 39 of his book (usually seen as the end of what is called First Isaiah) ends with his stark warning to king Hezekiah, 'Behold, the days come, that all that is in thine house... shall be carried to Babylon: nothing shall be left, saith the Lord'. Those words would have been spoken in the early years of the seventh century before Christ. In between Isaiah 39 and Isaiah 40 there is a gap of perhaps a hundred years, years of constant threat from the Assyrians and finally the all-conquering Babylonians, until Jerusalem was indeed conquered and ransacked and its people taken into slavery in 587BC. But God had not forgotten his people. He would send them a 'second Isaiah', another prophet of the same school, with a new message.

That is the background to the opening words of *Messiah*, which are taken from the first verse of chapter 40, the beginning of Second Isaiah—the story of the promise of God's eventual deliverance of his people, the story of a yet more distant and more splendid hope too, in the coming of that long-promised, long-expected Messiah.

Trials at an end

Comfort ye, comfort ye my people, saith your God. Speak ye comfortably to Jerusalem, and cry unto her, that her warfare is accomplished, that her iniquity is pardoned.

Isaiah 40:1–2

Messiah begins and ends with a voice: the voice of God begins the story, and the voice of angels ends it with a song of triumph. But triumph is still a long way away from these opening words, which are the first hints of better days for the people of Jerusalem.

It's sixty years on from the day when the Babylonian troops arrived and captured Jerusalem. Again, it's morning, and the city is rousing itself for business. After six decades of enemy occupation, they are losing hope that they will ever again be a free and independent people, or that their relatives who were marched off all those years ago to the slave camps of Babylon will ever return. They take little notice as the prophet makes his way to the stone steps—all that remains of the once magnificent temple of the Lord. He's a disciple of the great prophet Isaiah of a previous generation, and has taken the same name. They're used to his rantings and they know his message. 'It's all your fault. You ignored God, disobeyed his laws, turned to idols. It's all turned out exactly as we warned you it would!' Like the man on the modern street corner with the placard about 'the End of the World', they regard him as an irrelevance.

But today he surprises them. Usually his first word, shouted out above the noise of the market, is 'Woe!' Today—they can hardly believe their ears—it's 'Comfort!' People stop, tell their neighbours to listen, and wait to find out if they heard him correctly. Until today, his message has been a great deal more stick than carrot. But now, it seems, he has a new message. There's even a note of gentleness. At last, in all the despair and regret, there is hope.

God has told him, he says, to 'comfort' his people, to 'speak comfortably'—or as we would say now, 'tenderly'—to them. No one had spoken to them like that for sixty years—nothing but shouted commands from the occupiers and dire warnings from the prophets. Now, can they bring themselves to listen to a voice of comfort?

It's as though he is calling to them through a swirling mist, the sort of mist that has hung around for what has seemed an endless winter. He's speaking to a people who have been under a foreign yoke for so long that few of them have ever known freedom. Many of them have at last reluctantly come to accept that their fate is the just penalty of past failure and sin, that their God had every right to have punished them. But is it all too late? Has he abandoned them for ever?

It's against that setting that these words ring out, as they do in Handel's opening solo. The word 'Comfort' seems to hang in the air, its repetition like a divine echo. 'Comfort ye my people.' Were they really still 'my people', the covenant people of the one true God?

Isaiah was speaking to a nation torn between two conflicting emotions: despair and faith. Their plight seemed desperate and inescapable, yet they had always been told that 'their God'—the God of their forefathers, of Abraham, Isaac and Jacob—would never abandon them completely. Not only that, but in his own good time he would send them a saviour to lead them into a new era of hope, peace and prosperity.

This promised deliverer was known by the title Messiah, the 'anointed one'. It was applied to their kings, chosen by God and anointed with oil by the high priest. Messiah would be a king, too, but not like the kings they had experienced in their recent history. He would truly be God's chosen one, a fitting successor to the eternal throne of David, and the agent of God's purpose for his people. That was their 'messianic' hope.

And so the people of Judah waited, despair and faith competing, as they so often do in the experience of all God's people, then and now. The dark mist still enveloped them. There was no light on the horizon. But there comes a point where being told it's all our fault is not enough. And that point had now been reached. Jerusalem's time of 'warfare' was accomplished; her 'iniquity'— deep and persistent disobedience—was 'pardoned'. Indeed, in the biblical text, 'she hath received of the Lord's hand double for all her sins'. She had 'done her time', paid her debt. At last, her trials were at an end. God wanted to speak to her 'comfortably', 'tenderly'.

And that is always where true comfort lies. After all, we know about 'cold comfort' and 'false comfort', the voice that says 'it's all right now' when it clearly isn't. Real comfort is to receive strength from another (that's the origin of the word in English) but to receive it tenderly. For me, comfort is the person who doesn't simply put steel into your backbone, but also puts an arm around your shoulders. That, at last, was what the people of Jerusalem were being offered, and that is what God offers to any of his children who turn to him in their moment of despair.

A REFLECTION

God's comfort is, literally, his strength with us. It's not a warm and cosy feeling, but the confidence that he keeps his word and fulfils his promises. That confidence will often struggle with despair, but it rests on two great truths: God loves us, and we are his people.

The voice in the wilderness

The voice of him that crieth in the wilderness, Prepare ye the way of the Lord, make straight in the desert a highway for our God.

Isaiah 40:3

Lessons can be learnt in the wilderness that can never be learnt in the town. There different, quieter voices can be heard—voices that the rush of life drowns out.

The people of God, long enslaved, are to hear a voice. But it won't ring out in the streets of the capital. This voice can only be heard in the 'wilderness', the desert land to the east of Jerusalem, and still today a place of awesome heat, a stone-strewn landscape that looks something like the surface of the moon. There are no distractions there! In that setting, they could hear the voice of promise. The Lord was coming!

As we hear these words, full of such dramatic impact in their original setting for a captive people long ago, can they mean anything to us in our own situations? After all, we are not the people of Jerusalem awaiting deliverance from oppression and exile. But we are the people of the new covenant, and sometimes we, too, feel oppressed and exiled, at the mercy of the unbelieving world and even (so it seems) abandoned by our God. In us, too, despair sometimes wrestles with faith, and faith does not automatically have the victory.

In that situation, the words of Isaiah can come echoing through the mist of doubt. The Lord has not forgotten his promises and he has not abandoned his people. We are still his, as they were. He never makes people exiles from his family. Our iniquity is to be pardoned; our 'warfare'—for that is what it often feels like—is 'accomplished'. The price has been paid. The battle is over, at least for now. 'Prepare a way for the Lord.'

Like many children of my generation, I had a father who was quite strict. Just occasionally he would even take the slipper to us. But all through my childhood I never doubted two things: that he loved me, and that I was his son. It is the relationship that makes the difference. That was the lesson the people of Judah needed to learn. God might chide and correct them, but they must not doubt his love, or that they are his children.

But the voice of comfort is followed by the voice of warning. They are not incompatible, either for them or for us. If the Lord is to come to rescue us, then there is serious preparatory work to be done. The 'voice crying in the wilderness' says, 'Prepare ye the way of the Lord, make straight in the desert a highway for our God.' Obstacles will have to be removed, devious bends in our lives straightened out, a path cleared into the sovereign realms of our hearts, if the Saviour-Messiah of God is to come to us as our rescuer. And that process will occur more readily in the 'wilderness' than in the rush and bustle of everyday life.

For Handel and his collaborator, Charles Jennens, the connection with the coming of Jesus at the first Christmas was clear. They knew that John the Baptist was also 'a voice crying in the wilderness'—that same lonely and barren place above the Jordan valley. Just as Jerusalem had to prepare herself for the coming of God's salvation in Isaiah's day, so must the people of Judea 500 years later prepare themselves for the coming of the Messiah. John the Baptist used these very words, of course, as he called the people to get ready for the coming Saviour. Different places, different times, but one message: if the Lord is to come to us, we must prepare ourselves for his coming.

A REFLECTION

Sometimes we need to create space and quiet if we are to hear the voice of the Lord. Jesus spent forty days in the 'wilderness' being prepared for his ministry. St Paul spent a long while in 'the desert of Arabia' preparing for his. If we are to hear God's voice, sometimes we must take steps to shut out all the others!

Preparing the way

*Every valley shall be exalted, and every mountain and
hill made low: the crooked straight, and the rough places
plain.*

Isaiah 40:4

Before a highway of blessing can be built there is work to be done.
The ground must be cleared. Things that have stood in the way in
the past have to be removed. It is a consistent spiritual principle that
repentance leads to blessing, and the refusal to repent is the biggest
obstruction to it.

When a conquering king was about to enter a newly enslaved
kingdom it was customary to build a triumphal highway for his
victory procession. Boulders and trees would be removed, hillocks
flattened, wadis bridged, so that nothing would mar his moment
of triumph. Eventually he would appear in his chariot, flanked by
armed horsemen and ensign bearers, and with the miserable prisoners of war—and sometimes even the defeated king—bringing
up the rear. It was a flamboyant display of the fruits of victory.

Here, the prophet uses the same imagery in relation to the
arrival of the promised Messiah, God's conquering deliverer. If
the Lord was to come, then things must be made ready. Boulders,
trees, hills, valleys must not be allowed to delay his triumphal
progress. What is 'crooked' must be made 'straight' and what is
'rough' must be made 'plain'.

The imagery is not hard to interpret. The people who had so
signally failed to honour God in the past must change their ways
if things were to be different in the future. If they expected the
Lord to come and save them, then they must cooperate in his
purpose. The Messiah would not need, of course, a triumphal
highway like the tyrants of the ancient world, but he would
require a 'highway' into their consciences and attitudes. The boulders of sin, the rocks of disobedience, the mountains of idolatry,
the valleys of unbelief would all need to be eradicated. If the king
were to come, then his subjects must make themselves ready.

The choice of this particular prophecy at the beginning of the
'story' of *Messiah* is very apt. After all, John the Baptist applied

these very words to himself (Mark 1:3). The one who prepared the way for the Messiah, Jesus, had a message very similar to Isaiah's. If you want to welcome the Messiah-Saviour, then do some inward preparation now. Remove the sins that have delayed his coming. Turn from disobedience, idolatry and unbelief. John's word was the unambiguous command, 'Repent!' It means, 'Have a complete change of attitude... start a new life... reject the sins that have brought you to your present condition... Turn back to God.'

Sadly, the people of Isaiah's day found this beyond them. God did, in his mercy, eventually deliver them from the Babylonians, but he used a heathen king, Cyrus, rather than a divine Messiah to achieve it. Their repentance was neither true enough nor deep enough to testify to a genuine change of heart. Consequently, the hope of a Messiah to restore the glory of Israel remained unfulfilled

Indeed, when the Messiah eventually came—500 years and more after Judah and Jerusalem were eventually set free from the Babylonian yoke—the people of Israel were yet again in captivity, and had been so for no less than 300 years. First the Greeks and then the Romans had taken away their sovereignty and subjected them to Gentile laws and Gentile ways. The 'highway' had still not been properly prepared. The same spiritual obstacles remained, and still needed to be cleared away. It was John the Baptist's ministry to 'prepare the way', and that involved the same message of repentance and obedience that the great prophets of Israel had proclaimed, and which the people had chosen to reject.

In one sense, nothing changes. The path to blessing is still the way of repentance. The Saviour's approach is still obstructed by the debris of sin and disobedience. The call is still to 'prepare the way of the Lord'.

A REFLECTION

John the Baptist's message of repentance and baptism prepared people for the coming of Jesus Christ, God's Messiah, at a particular moment in history. But day by day he comes to us, too, along the same highway, and part of our discipleship is to keep it clear of obstructions.

4

For all to see

*And the glory, the glory of the Lord shall be revealed, and all
flesh shall see it together: for the mouth of the Lord hath
spoken it.*

Isaiah 40:5

*Thus saith the Lord, the Lord of hosts; Yet once, a little
while, and I will shake the heavens, and the earth, the sea
and the dry land; And I will shake all nations, and the desire
of all nations shall come.*

Haggai 2:6–7

*The Lord, whom ye seek, shall suddenly come to his temple,
even the messenger of the covenant, whom ye delight in:
behold, he shall come, saith the Lord of hosts.*

Malachi 3:1

Jesus said that the second 'coming of the Son of Man' would be like
a flash of lightning, visible from one horizon to the other. At times,
God acts in secret, inward ways, but the first arrival of the Messiah
was also to be a public event, proclaimed by angels, good news 'for
all the people'.

In the text of *Messiah* Charles Jennens occasionally brings together scripture in a way that would give modern biblical scholars a fit!
By the strict canons of interpretation, you aren't supposed to take
a text from here and a text from there—written at different times
by different people, for different 'audiences'—and paste them
together to make a whole. Yet, given any kind of belief in the
inspiration of scripture, this kind of 'kangaroo exegesis' (as it has
been cruelly described) can actually be very enlightening. And
this, for me, is a splendid example!

Jennens starts with the promise of Isaiah that the 'glory of the
Lord' will be revealed, to be seen by 'all flesh'. In other words, a
day was coming when the divine glory, what the Israelites knew as
the *shekinah*, the visible evidence of the presence of God in the

midst of his covenant people, would be seen by everybody. This would happen on the day of God's deliverance, when he would answer the prayers and longings of his people and vindicate them before the whole world.

The *shekinah* is a rather mysterious concept. Back in the days of the exodus 'something' assured the people of Israel that God was with them. As they marched there was a pillar of cloud, which also settled over the tabernacle when they halted. At the dedication of the temple by Solomon, there came a moment when 'the glory of the Lord had filled the house of the Lord' (1 Kings 8:11). Whatever this 'glory' was, it was highly visible; people knew it had 'happened'. It was a sign you could see—a cloud, or a brightness, perhaps—which confirmed the presence of the Lord. Perhaps the *shekinah* is the nearest thing in the Old Testament to the New Testament concept of the Holy Spirit as God's conspicuous presence among his people.

Anyway, the 'glory' of the Lord would be seen. 'All flesh' would witness God's deliverance of his people. This would be no secret operation: enemy as well as friend would recognize that God was at work.

Jennens then moves on to words of Haggai which make a similar promise to the people of Jerusalem in the following generation. They are trying to rebuild the temple which had been laid waste by the Babylonians, but from time to time they lose heart. What is this temple compared with the glory of Solomon's? And who are they, a tiny band of former prisoners of war, in a world of mighty international powers? Haggai's answer is that 'in a little while' the Lord will come and 'shake all nations' and then 'fill this house'—the one they were rebuilding—with 'glory'. Then the nations would see!

The third passage is from Malachi, yet another generation or two further on. Again, it is the same promise: I will send my messenger, preparing the way for an even greater one, 'the Lord whom ye seek'. He will come suddenly, when you don't expect him, to the temple of God.

Three prophets, three different generations, three different historical contexts—but one message, as Jennens suggested. They all speak of the 'glory of the Lord', the visible divine presence. Visibility was its distinctive quality. Israel had seen it in the past, chosen individuals had seen it in their day, but now the whole earth would see the Lord's glory in one mighty revelation: 'the glory of the Lord shall be revealed'—hidden no longer, no nation's private possession any longer, but for all to see. And that glory would be revealed in the coming of a person, the Lord's 'messenger', the one they had been seeking for so long. Indeed, there is a hint in Malachi's prophecy that the one who was to come would be none other than 'the Lord' himself. In other words, when the Messiah came, so would the glory of the Lord: and the whole earth would be witness to it.

So the story of the coming Messiah inches forward. The one they are waiting for will come, and when he does it will be glorious, visible and public.

A REFLECTION

Sometimes Christians feel that they are rather a despised minority! Indeed, in the face of the tidal wave of commerce, or the confidence of science, or the pride of materialism, we may be tempted to doubt God's ultimate sovereignty over all things. It sometimes seems God only works invisibly! Yet whenever God 'comes', when his day arrives, his actions are powerful and visible. They were during the life of Jesus—and they will be, finally and irrefutably, when he comes again and 'every eye shall see him'.

5

The refiner's fire

But who may abide the day of his coming? and who shall
stand when he appeareth? for he is like a refiner's fire.

Malachi 3:2

And he shall purify the sons of Levi that they may offer unto
the Lord an offering in righteousness.

Malachi 3:3

There is a question to be asked and answered before we are ready to welcome the coming of the Lord: who could survive under the searchlight of his purity?

It is one thing for the glory of the Lord to be revealed; it's quite another to ask ourselves how we would react if he appeared to us. After all, when God 'came down' to meet Moses on Mount Sinai to deliver the Ten Commandments, it was a scene of indescribable awe—smoke, thunder, earthquakes—and no one except Moses was permitted even to touch the mountain. God's presence is a 'consuming fire'; he dwells in 'unapproachable light'. So while it is marvellous to think that the Lord might reveal himself on earth, it is also a sobering thought. How can we hope to stand in his presence?

Hence we have these words of the prophet Malachi, placed after words of hope and promise of the Messiah's coming, and (in *Messiah*) immediately before the narrative of the birth of Jesus. 'The Lord whom ye seek shall suddenly come to his temple'... 'but who may abide the day of his coming?' We should never ignore the 'buts' of scripture!

In one sense the prophet answers his own question. The Messiah when he comes will come as a 'refiner' of silver and gold. It was a familiar image in the ancient world, where the precious metals were heated in a dish over an intensely hot fire until all the dross and impurities were burnt away and all that was left was pure gold or pure silver. St Peter uses the same imagery in his New Testament letter, where he sees the sufferings of Christian believers as being part of this process of 'refinement'. They were being 'tested [refined] with fire' (1 Peter 1:7).

In the full biblical text the 'Lord's messenger' is also likened to 'fullers' soap', the bleaching agent used in the laundry in those days. He will himself be the agent of cleansing, the refiner who removes all the impurity and dross and makes it possible for creatures like ourselves to stand before their incarnate Creator.

'And he shall purify the sons of Levi.' As so often, the process of repentance and cleansing needed to begin in the holiest place of all, the temple, and with the men who were charged to carry out the holiest functions, the priests of the Lord. So the 'sons of Levi', the members of the priestly tribe of Israel, would be the first to experience the Messiah's refining and cleansing action. Only when they had been 'purified' would they be able to offer sacrifices 'in righteousness'—that is, with clean hands and pure hearts.

When I was a choir-boy, it used to baffle me that we always began our services by telling God how sinful we were. Then we would say how sorry this made us, and after that we would all be told that God forgave us. Fair enough, I supposed. But next week we were all back saying exactly the same thing again. Didn't we ever get any better?

I remember our vicar explaining to me that the nearer you came to God the more aware you were of how 'unclean' your life was. So when we came to church to worship God—to 'stand in his presence', as we say—it was more than ever necessary to admit our faults and ask to be made clean. As he put it, 'You wouldn't barge into dinner with the King at Windsor Castle with dirty hands, now would you?'

I saw his point. In much the same way, if we believe that the Lord is coming to us, the proper response is to 'wash ourselves', to cleanse our hearts and minds. These words in *Messiah* make precisely that point. We should not take the coming of the Lord lightly. In past ages Christians spent much of Advent in heart-searching and self-examination as a preparation for celebrating the nativity of the Saviour and his future coming in judgment. It's perhaps typical of our less serious approach to such things that Advent has simply become for many people 'the run-up to Christmas'. Yet it is as true now as it was in the days of Malachi that the only proper preparation for standing in the presence of a holy God is the refining fire of his holiness and the cleansing from impurity and dross.

If I am to welcome the birth of the Messiah, I need to recognize who he is—the incarnation of holiness and purity—and my need of his refining and cleansing work. We associate many emotions with Christmas—fun, laughter, celebration, joy… but can we add another set of emotions: awe, reverence, wonder, repentance? Perhaps only those who get that balance right can truly be said to be ready for 'the day of his coming'.

THE BIRTH OF THE MESSIAH

Handel's *Messiah* confines the libretto of the birth of Jesus to just two biblical sources, the prophet Isaiah and the evangelist Luke. The first provides the prophetic background to the birth of the Messiah; the second, in memorable words, tells the story of the event.

When Isaiah spoke of the child who would be born, or of the light that would dawn, or of the mighty king who would rescue his people, he was certainly not thinking—consciously, at least—of the birth of a child hundreds of years later in Bethlehem, or of a saviour who would die a criminal's death on a cross. It is of the nature of prophetic language that it can bear many levels of meaning and be interpreted in different ways at different times. After all, a vision is a vision, not a prediction.

So it is not surprising that Christians from the very dawn of the Church have turned to the prophecies of Isaiah and found in them marvellous insights into the meaning of the coming of Jesus. He was called 'the Christ', which is simply the Greek word for 'Messiah', the Anointed One. That very title makes the link with all the messianic language and concepts of the Old Testament, and nowhere is that language more rich and profound—or apparently more appropriate to the ministry of Jesus—than in the book of Isaiah.

Messiah sets the story of the birth of Jesus against a stark contrast of darkness and light. It is the same contrast that Isaiah saw in his own day. When things are at their blackest and human hope is at its lowest level, the God of grace moves in salvation and renewal. It is the imagery of the opening chapters of John's Gospel—'the light shone in the darkness'. As the old saying puts it: 'the night is darkest just before the dawn'.

Every Christmas the words of Isaiah are read at our services of Lessons and Carols, so that they have become inextricably linked with the birth of the Messiah Jesus—almost to the extent that people are shocked to be told that in their original context they may well have applied to this or that historical figure of that time. Yet the multi-layered nature of prophecy means that there is no exclusive interpretation of the prophet's words. They could be true then, and again at the coming of Jesus, and again at the second coming. Indeed, in one sense if they are true and inspired by

God, their truth can never be contained in one event or one moment of history. They are simply true for all time: timeless light shining in universal darkness.

6

God with us

Behold, a virgin shall conceive, and bear a son, and shall call his name Emmanuel, God with us.

Matthew 1:23 *(quoting Isaiah 7:14)*

Whenever God comes to us, there is a moment of judgment. Do we welcome him and obey his voice? Or do we fail to recognize who it is who has come?

As soon as one reads Isaiah's passage in its context, it is obvious that whatever else the prophet had in mind it was not the birth of a saviour. At a time of great tension in Judah, the king, Ahaz, had declined to ask the Lord for a sign, but Isaiah told him that nevertheless a sign would be given him. That sign would be the birth of a special child, a child of great spiritual insight and judgment ('he may know to refuse the evil, and choose the good'). But this baby, born to a 'young woman' (or 'virgin', the words were virtually synonymous) would not come as a saviour but as a sign of God's judgment. Before the child would be fully grown up the Lord would bring on the people of Judah the most terrible of all the potential invading powers, the king of Assyria (see Isaiah 7:15–17).

So are we right—was *Messiah* right—to apply this prophecy to the birth of the Saviour, Jesus? The angel told Joseph that this child was to be 'Emmanuel', God with us. Clearly that was a promise of great comfort and hope. Yet in context this prophecy speaks of a child who will judge a disobedient people, not save them.

To understand what this particular scripture tells us we must go back to the words of Malachi in the last section. The coming of the Lord's anointed is an occasion for judgment as well as hope. These words of Isaiah tell us that God is with us in our moments of judgment as well as in our need for salvation. In other words, 'Emmanuel' is not just a title of comfort, but also of challenge. Those whom God is 'with' are bearers of a responsibility. As Malachi saw, he has to be recognized and obeyed. His coming demands righteousness and purity. Sadly, the child Isaiah spoke of here—a prophetic symbol, probably, rather than an actual person—was born to a people whose eyes were closed to the message: they didn't recognize the hand of God in his coming. The 'sign' which could have saved Judah served instead to judge them.

This prophecy of Isaiah has become part of the story of the birth of the Messiah Jesus because Matthew made the identification. In the course of reassuring Joseph about Mary's pregnancy, the angel who appeared to him 'in a dream' said that it had come about to fulfil what was 'spoken of the Lord by the prophet'—and he quoted these words from Isaiah. The child was to be called 'Jesus: for he shall save his people from their sins' ('Jesus' means 'saviour'), yet the prophecy says that 'they shall call his name Emmanuel' (which means 'God with us'). To the best of our knowledge, Jesus was never called 'Emmanuel', but of course the unfolding story of the Gospel reveals him to be precisely what 'Emmanuel' means—God present among his people.

The other question about this prophecy concerns the use of the word 'virgin'. The word used by Isaiah could mean any young, unmarried woman, which in the social climate of the time was much the same as saying 'virgin'. On the other hand, the Greek word used by Matthew, and also by Luke (1:27), unambiguously means 'virgin', in the biological sense. This has led some critics to suggest that the concept of the virgin birth of Jesus was read into the New Testament story from a misunderstood Old Testament prophecy.

The argument might have some relevance where Matthew is concerned. But Luke does not so much as mention the prophecy of Isaiah, yet the virginity of Mary is central to his birth narrative, from her astonished response to the angel Gabriel ('How can this be, since I am a virgin?') to the angelic reply that she would be with child by 'the Holy Spirit'. For Luke, at least, the virginal conception of Jesus is not so much a fulfilment of prophecy as a part of the event.

For the Christian, the title 'Emmanuel' has, in any case, a special and unique value. It describes precisely what we understand the incarnation to mean: that for a season God himself dwelt among us. As St John put it, rather more poetically, 'The Word became flesh and pitched his tent among us' (a literal translation of John 1:14).

When God comes among us there are always and only two possible consequences: judgment or salvation. There is judgment, if we close our eyes to his coming, or refuse to receive him. In that case, we are dependent on God's justice and mercy. Or there is salvation and healing if we welcome him with faith and trust.

The bringer of good news

O thou that tellest good tidings to Zion, get thee up into the high mountain; lift up thy voice with strength; lift it up, be not afraid; say unto the cities of Judah, Behold your God! Arise, shine, for thy light is come, and the glory of the Lord is risen upon thee.

Isaiah 40:9; 60:1

A promise of light only makes sense to those at present in darkness—but the darker it is, the more brightly shines the light.

Both of these commands are addressed to the people of God, the residents of the Holy Land and the Holy City, Zion (Jerusalem). In the text of Isaiah 'Zion' is told to 'get up into the high mountain' with the good news and 'Jerusalem' is to lift up her voice with strength. In other words, this is good news for all the people, and all the people should join in passing it on. There are pre-echoes here, of course, of the message of the angels at the birth of Jesus— 'good news... for all the people'.

In the second, later quotation (from Isaiah 60), the people are told to witness to the Gentiles too (v. 3), that the time of the coming of the light has arrived, the day of the Lord's 'glory'.

The words are well chosen. As we have seen already, God's purpose is to reveal his glory to the whole world. What had been a private or national possession was to become the joy of the whole earth. The news that God was moving to free and bless his people was to be proclaimed from the mountains—we'd say, 'from the roof-tops'.

But there was a fear to be overcome—'be not afraid'. And there always is in the process of proclaiming good news. After all, 'good news' for Judah was presumably 'bad news' for her enemies and oppressors. Not only that, but to shout about good news draws attention to us. Wouldn't it be altogether wiser to keep a low profile and simply let God get on with it?

I was speaking at a church meeting about the need for Christians to 'go public' about their faith—to 'proclaim it from the roof-tops'. Perhaps I was a bit too enthusiastic! Anyway, a smartly dressed man sitting at the back remarked that he had always believed his faith was 'a private matter between him and God'.

I could only agree, at one level. Of course our faith is a private and personal commitment, known (in its interior sincerity) only to God. But I pointed out, as courteously as I could, that it was just as well the apostles hadn't taken that view, because if they had the Christian faith would have died out in about AD80 when the last of them toppled off his chair in the upper room wondering if they shouldn't have told somebody that Jesus had risen from the dead.

In other words, what was true for Judah two and a half thousand years ago is still true for us. We know that we have been given good news, and commanded to share it—indeed, to shout it from the roof-tops. But the voice of fear and hesitation intrudes. Would that really be wise? Should we draw such public attention to ourselves? Isn't the work of God secret, personal, private to each of us, far too 'precious' to be the subject of noisy proclamation?

As a consequence, the 'good news' of God's glory revealed through his Son is not so much shouted as stifled. It's as though we are somehow ashamed of the sheer blatancy of God's action in coming among us. 'Lift up thy voice with strength', urges Isaiah, 'Lift it up, do not be afraid.' There are times when silence is golden, but there are also times when silence is gutless.

In any case, to hide light is to defeat its very reason for being. As Jesus said, people don't light a lamp and put it under a bowl. In the same way, he urged, 'Let your light shine before others'. The moment of God's salvation is not the time for secrecy!

A REFLECTION

The people of God of the Old Covenant were to be the bearers of good news and bringers of light to the world, but found that calling difficult and unattractive. It's also true that many Christians, the people of the New Covenant, find it hard to share their faith with others. Yet we, too, have good news for the whole world—and good news is meant to be shared, not kept to ourselves.

Light for the nations

For, behold, darkness shall cover the earth, and gross
darkness the people: but the Lord shall arise upon thee, and
his glory shall be seen upon thee. And the Gentiles shall come
to thy light, and kings to the brightness of thy rising.

Isaiah 60:2–3

As the darkest of nights draws to a close, the sun begins to push up
over the eastern horizon. Soon its light is dispelling the last vestiges
of night. A new day has dawned.

As a kind of 'overture' to the climax of the birth of the Messiah,
Handel offers us a pastiche of light and darkness. The teller of
good news has climbed to the mountain-top, but below him
stretch in darkness the lands as yet enslaved. The call is for God's
people to bear the light to the nations, but the flame has not yet
lit up their own lives. Here the reminder is of the darkness—
'gross', thick darkness—that overlays not only the enslaved children of the covenant but the 'nations', the Gentiles who have
enslaved them. The promise is that light will come, but until the
moment of dawning all that is visible is darkness.

In its historical context, this speaks of the moment when the
heathen nations who have conquered and terrorized 'the people'
(that is, the people of God) will have to recognize the glory of the
God of Israel as he moves in power to deliver the oppressed and
overthrow the armies of the Gentiles. When the light of God's
glory dawns, in other words, the whole world will have to recognize it. Even 'kings' will bow the knee as the Sun of Righteousness
rises in the east. Perhaps there is a hint here of the conquering
rulers of the Gentiles being brought into Jerusalem as captives in
chains. It will be a moment of vindication. God was right after all.
Even the greatest human power has to acknowledge his justice
and might.

In its prophetic context, the words speak of a great truth about
God. He is the source of light—of truth and justice and righteousness. In the long run, his purposes are fulfilled, even though
sometimes his people doubt it, or are impatient at what they see
as his 'delays'. Yet at the proper time, according to his purpose,

'the Lord will arise', his 'glory will be seen'. And when he comes, the whole world will be invited to share in the 'brightness of his rising' (that is, to enjoy the bright light of dawn). From the earliest days of the Church, Christians have seen a fulfilment of this in the story of the Eastern magi—whom they regarded as Gentile 'kings'—bringing their worship to the infant Jesus.

For us, in our own everyday life of faith, these are also eternal truths. Who has never felt impatient at what we see as God's 'delays'? Why does he seem indifferent to our prayers, slow to answer and reluctant to intervene? And why does he seem to stand by while his Church and Gospel are blasphemed and his followers persecuted or ridiculed? It is the same test of faith as Isaiah recognized, and the answer is also the same. God will act, but in his own time. He will 'grant justice to his chosen ones who cry to him day and night' (Luke 18:7), but at the time of his appointment. He does hear, he does care, and the light will dawn. 'The light shines in the darkness, and the darkness did not overcome it' (John 1:5).

A REFLECTION

The people of Judah had to wait for 50 years for the liberation of Jerusalem in 538BC. At the time of the birth of Jesus, the Jews had been under foreign occupation for 300 years. In both cases, faith was wearing thin! Yet God fulfilled his promises. Jerusalem was set free and the temple rebuilt. The Messiah did come, with news of a new kingdom, the kingdom of God. How would we respond to people today who ask the old, old question, 'Where is your God? Why doesn't he do something?'

The land of shadows

The people that walked in darkness have seen a great light:
and they that dwell in the land of the shadow of death, upon
them hath the light shined.

Isaiah 9:2

**Death is the shadow that darkens every human joy, the spectre that
lurks at every human feast. A light that can lift that shadow would
be the greatest of all gifts.**

In the swelling overture to the moment when the birth of the
Messiah occurs, this solo provides a sombre counterpoint. The
blessing that is to come is specifically for those who have been
walking in darkness. In the beautiful 'parallelism' of Hebrew poet-
ry (where each new idea is echoed in parallel imagery) that image
of those 'that walked in darkness' is elaborated as 'they that dwell
in the land of the shadow of death', a reminder of the familiar
words of Psalm 23. The great light is for those who have experienced great darkness.

The previous verse of Isaiah tells us that 'there will be no gloom
for those who were in anguish'... in the future the Lord will honour 'the way of the sea, the land along the Jordan, Galilee of the
nations'. Galilee, as is clear from the Gospels, was a rather
despised region of Israel, being regarded as a place where
Gentiles settled alongside Jews, yet it is picked out here for the
special blessing, the coming of the 'great light'. That has particular meaning for Christians, of course, who know that Jesus was
conceived and grew up in that very Galilee and that it was there,
in the Jordan, that he was baptized and there, along the sea-side
of the lake, that he began his ministry of miracle and message.

In its context, this passage seems almost contradictory. It comes
between two passages of stern warning, the first of judgment at
the hands of the king of Assyria (Isaiah 8:6–8) and the second of
judgment on the leaders, elders and rulers of Israel, who had
misled the people and taught them lies (Isaiah 9:12–16). Yet in
between them is this oracle of hope, looking on to a time in the
future when the 'yoke of their burden' (Isaiah 9:4) will be
shattered.

In the case of the people of Judah and Jerusalem, that 'yoke' was one of physical oppression, but the word 'darkness' hints at deeper and less tangible problems. The people are 'walking in darkness'; they 'dwell in the land of the shadow of death'—the ultimate 'darkness'. A great liberator might indeed overthrow the Assyrians, who had been threatening and oppressing them for a long while, but he could not deliver them from the ultimate oppressor, death itself.

The exact meaning of Isaiah's words is not clear to today's reader, partly because the Jewish beliefs about death and resurrection at this time are quite hard to establish. But there is no doubt that for them, as for us, death was the final enemy, the shadow that hung over the whole of life—what Lord Coggan, once called 'the skeleton in everyone's cupboard'.

In that sense, we all 'dwell in the land of the shadow of death', and there could be no promise more splendid than that the 'great light' of God should illuminate its landscape. As a parish priest I have spent many hours with people who know that they are approaching death. More than the rest of us, who can push such thoughts to the back of our minds, they are aware that they are citizens of the Land of the Shadow.

What is indescribably wonderful is to see how, time and again, the 'great light' has shone for them, so that the pathway which had seemed so gloomy becomes a way of light and life. For them, this prophecy has been fulfilled in a remarkable way. 'They that dwell in the land of the shadow of death, upon them hath the light shined.' Victory over the fear of death is a greater triumph than the conquest of the Assyrian hordes!

A REFLECTION

All of us, at some time sooner or later, will walk through the land of the shadow. The 'great light' that is promised there is, as we shall see, the 'wonderful child' who is to be born. And the reason he can shine light into that particular dark place is that he has been there for us, and now comes to us as the Lord of life and conqueror of death.

Child of promise

For unto us a child is born, unto us a son is given: and the government shall be upon his shoulder: and his name shall be called Wonderful, Counsellor, The mighty God, The everlasting Father, The Prince of Peace.

Isaiah 9:6

Some children seem destined from birth for greatness. But of none but this one could such divine qualities have been foretold. This child is to be God-like.

The event is still kept tantalizingly in the future, as though Handel and Jennens want us to be clear how important and revolutionary it will be when it occurs. The prophetic message holds out such astonishing hopes that they want us to savour them to the full, like children anticipating a treat. Here words of Isaiah about a promised child are used as the climax of the prelude, if one can put it that way. After this, the voice of prophecy is stilled and the voice of history speaks.

By any account, and however we interpret it, this is an amazing prophecy. In its context, it speaks of the birth of a child 'for' the people of Judah ('unto us'), to come in their time of greatest need and greatest weakness and demonstrate the very power and authority of God. For this 'child'—in sharp contrast to the usual role of infants—would have authority: the 'government' would be 'upon his shoulders'—he would bear its weight.

And he would be wise, again in a way that children are not expected to be—a 'counsellor', one whose advice is weighty and profound. He would have God-like power. That seems to be the meaning of 'The mighty God' (no Jew could have conceived of a human baby being itself Yahweh, the 'mighty God'). He would, though a child, have the qualities of a father, protective and caring, providing for his people. And he would be a 'Prince'—not the warrior-prince with which they were familiar, but a 'Prince of Peace'.

For those who heard the original prophecy of Isaiah, this would have been a picture of a coming potential Saviour-King who would shatter 'the yoke' that burdened the people (see Isaiah 9:4) and bring in a new reign of justice, righteousness and peace. It was a lovely vision, but one has to say that, in strictly historical terms, it never happened. The people were eventually delivered from slavery, but by a pagan king, not a heaven-sent Messiah. At the end of the Old Testament era, the prophets are still looking forward to the time when such a 'child' would be born.

So it is not surprising that Christians have always seen in this prophecy a vision that was only to become a reality at Bethlehem, in the birth of Jesus Christ. All of the qualities of this child of prophecy came to their fulfilment in him and (to be honest) only in him. He would be born 'for us'. He would have authority in himself. He would speak the wisest words ever to come from the lips of a human being. He would be God-like in his power, over disease, the elements, even death itself. He would protect and provide for his followers, like a father, feeding them with 'bread from heaven'. He would be the supreme 'Prince of Peace'—as St Paul said, 'making peace through the blood of his cross' (Colossians 1:20).

These prophetic words, spoken to a frightened and threatened people in one of the darkest periods of Jerusalem's tortured history, offer for the Christian believer a beautiful picture of the Saviour-Messiah, who came to free us from sin and death, to make peace between humankind and God, and to 'open the kingdom of heaven to all believers'.

So the stage is set. The vision has been announced. From the hot streets of Jerusalem in the seventh century BC we move to the pastoral calm of the hills around the little town of Bethlehem nearly 700 years later.

A REFLECTION

There is a marvellous paradox in the idea that all of the wisdom, power, authority and strength of God are to be found in... a child. But what a child speaks of is potential, and of no child can that be more true than the one who is the Son of his Father.

11

The promised Saviour

There were shepherds abiding in the field, keeping watch over their flock by night. And, lo, the angel of the Lord came upon them, and the glory of the Lord shone round about them: and they were sore afraid. And the angel said unto them, Fear not: for, behold, I bring you good tidings of great joy, which shall be to all people. For unto you is born this day in the city of David a Saviour, which is Christ the Lord.

Luke 2:8–11

God can and does reveal the most marvellous things to ordinary people, going about their ordinary lives—provided they have ears and eyes open to what is happening.

To someone who didn't already know the plot, the preamble to the birth of the Messiah seems to hit an anti-climax in the event itself. Borne along by splendid words, great promises and the music of anticipated glory, we have been brought to the moment 'by prophets long foretold'. But when we get there, how does the story start? 'There were shepherds…'

Shepherds were near the bottom of the social pile in ancient Israel. This was not so much because of the nature of their work but because it precluded them from sharing in the necessary religious rites and rituals. They couldn't leave their sheep, so they were unable to get to synagogue or temple. They could not join in the prayers, hear the Law, or offer their sacrifices. Their lives were totally dedicated to their flocks. They 'abided' in the fields, in the lovely language of the King James Bible—in other words, they lived there, the fields were their 'abode'. Tourists to Bethlehem are still shown a shepherds' cave, where these hardy men endured cold nights 'watching over their flocks'.

So it was no wonder that Jesse, when the prophet Samuel came in search of a future king from among his sons, was reluctant to admit that the youngest was out on the hills, 'keeping the sheep' (1 Samuel 16:11). This was no task for a future monarch! Yet it was that young shepherd boy, David, who became Israel's greatest king, the one from whose descendants would be drawn 'great David's greater son', the Messiah.

And Bethlehem was 'the city of David' (v. 11). To that very place Joseph—'of the house and lineage of David'—had brought his pledged wife, Mary, 'being great with child'. In the place where David grew up his great successor was to be born, and on the hills where he once tended the sheep the shepherds of this later time were to be the first to learn of the birth of the Messiah. The whole story has a wonderful completeness about it, as though to make it clear to us that this was no accident but the fulfilment of an intricate and meticulous plan and purpose.

So the shepherds, ordinary people going about their ordinary business, were startled by a series of totally unexpected events. An 'angel of the Lord' appeared. The 'glory of the Lord'—that *shekinah* glory of which the prophet Isaiah spoke—shone around them. The dark night was illuminated by the very presence of God. No wonder they were 'sore afraid'!

And the message, when it came, was no less startling. They were the recipients of 'good news' ('glad tidings') of 'great joy'—a joy that was 'for all the people'. The message, in other words, was to them, but they were to receive it on behalf of the whole people of Israel. Quite a responsibility! When they heard what it was, the magnitude of it may have escaped them at that moment. For this was no less than the moment their nation had been praying for, awaiting with a hope and expectation that years of disappointment had slowly eroded. God had heard the prayers of his people. The moment of their salvation was at hand. The long-promised Messiah had been born.

'For to you is born this day in the city of David a Saviour, which is Christ the Lord.' 'Christ', as we have seen, is simply the Greek form of the Hebrew word 'Messiah', the Anointed One. The announcement could not have been more stark and clear. The Messiah has been born, to be the Saviour of his people. And this handful of social outcasts on the hills were the first people on earth to know about it.

They were given a 'sign', to enable them to identify this particular baby. They might have expected that he would be wearing royal robes and lying in the arms of a princess. But in fact he would be found wearing 'swaddling cloths'—the simple linen bandages with which poor people bound up the new-born infant—and lying in a feeding trough.

The whole scene is one that turns normal expectations upside down. It would be an exaggeration to say that the birth of Jesus took place in squalid circumstances, as I have heard some preachers claim. By the standards of the time there was nothing squalid about a birth in a place where cattle were kept—every rural home would have recognized the scene. But it was a setting of utter simplicity, shorn of anything that would suggest rank, power or wealth. It was the birth of a child to a simple, peasant couple in a simple, rural setting.

And the shepherds fit perfectly into this scenario. They pursued an honourable trade, but a poor and often despised one. They were on the fringes of the society of Israel, not quite outlaws but strangers to the usual niceties of custom and religion. They waited on the hills, while the conventionally devout (like Anna and Simeon—see Luke 2:21–38) waited for the Messiah in the temple. But it was to the shepherds that the angel appeared with his message, and it was shepherds who bore the first news of the birth of Israel's Saviour into the streets of David's ancestral town. The 'devout' got their revelation later!

God still has marvellous things to say to ordinary people. He is still, in the old biblical phrase, 'no respecter of persons'. The birth of Jesus is a wonderful reminder that intellect, rank, social position, worldly power and reputation cut no ice with God. The shepherds never forgot the needs of their sheep, and God never forgot the needs of the shepherds.

A REFLECTION

Sheer familiarity can blunt the sharp edge of this story. Try to visualize the scene as Luke describes it and put yourself into the position of the shepherds. Hear the words for the first time. Experience the shock, the surprise, the awe which they would have evoked. And then set out with them to Bethlehem to 'see this thing that has taken place' (Luke 2:15).

Hymn of blessing

And suddenly there was with the angel a multitude of the heavenly host praising God, and saying, Glory to God in the highest, and peace on earth, good will toward men.

Luke 2:13–14

The birth of Jesus had two immediate consequences. It brought glory to God in heaven, because his purpose had been fulfilled. And it brought the possibility of peace on earth, because the divine bringer of peace had arrived.

The angels' song has been a part of Christian hymnody from the earliest days of the Church, and these words are still sung Sunday by Sunday in the Gloria. For Handel they are a sudden and spectacular eruption of praise, the notes cascading down, as though the glory was pouring from heaven to the fields and streets of earth, and then up again as the words 'Glory to God' are repeated, the song which began in heaven returning there in praise to the Creator.

And indeed the song has two audiences. It is of 'glory to God' in 'the highest' (that is, in the highest reaches of heaven) and of 'peace on earth' (that is, for all the people and nations of the world). It swings low, and it swoops up high!

The words are simple and very, very well known, but they are actually very difficult to translate, as is obvious if you try looking them up in half a dozen different Bible versions. The trouble is that phrase 'good will toward men'. The RSV translates it 'Peace among men with whom he is pleased'. The REB has 'Peace to all in whom he delights'. The NIV offers 'Peace to men on whom his favour rests'. Each of those translations seems to imply a restriction. This is not 'universal' good will from God to the human race, but just to a favoured few.

The word used by Luke, *eudokias*, speaks of God's goodwill to us, not our goodwill to him or to others. Here, it is 'goodwill toward men'. In the New Testament generally *eudokias* and its derivatives invariably means 'favoured'—'those who enjoy God's favour'. But that does not imply that some don't, or are excluded from it. I believe that the angels' message promised 'peace on earth to people who (now) enjoy God's favour'—all people, everywhere.

The coming of Jesus heralds a new era in which peace will be possible in all the fundamental relationships: between people, between races and nations and, most importantly of all, between humanity and its Creator. 'Peace' in the Jewish understanding—expressed in the beautiful word *shalom*—means wholeness, the state of life which corresponds to the will of God. It is 'well-being' in contrast to evil. It is security in place of fear. Peace, in this sense, was always an essential ingredient of the messianic hope, as we saw in the prophecies of Isaiah. The Messiah would be the 'Prince of Peace'.

When this peace is present, there is glory to God. God is glorified when his people live in a state of 'wholeness', when their circumstances correspond to the will of God. Sin and evil took away that priceless 'wholeness', but now, in the coming of Jesus, it may be restored. The Saviour will 'save his people from their sins'. He will heal their wounds and make them whole. In that way, God's favour and kindness will be revealed on earth.

Human history has revealed what a fragile prize peace is. In modern political jargon we like to speak of a 'peace process', recognizing that peace is not a 'thing' that you can acquire but a condition into which we need to enter. Peace, in that sense, is much, much more than the absence of war. It is a state of well-being in which humanity can flourish as God intended. That it is so elusive that all of us can only speak of it as a future hope, shows how little humanity has heeded the message of the angels on the first Christmas. Peace on earth is the consequence of God's goodwill to us, recognized and received, a response to his undeserved love and kindness. And peace brings glory not only on earth but in the 'highest heavens'.

A REFLECTION

We may not be in a position to create peace between nations or races, but we can begin where we are to pray and work for that state of being which corresponds to God's will in our own circumstances. We can also open ourselves to his favour and kindness, so that our lives have within them his gift of peace.

THE LIFE OF THE MESSIAH

The opening 'movement' of *Messiah* combines hope and warning. Both the words and the music have a prophetic quality, sometimes whispering, sometimes shouting. Later, when the story of redemption through the cross is to be told, the music will again range across the emotions. But this second 'movement', which paints in pastel colours the life of the Messiah, Jesus, has an air of calm and pastoral tenderness. It speaks of peace, healing, security, of burdens lifted and blind eyes opened. No wonder Jesus' arrival was introduced with a 'pastoral symphony'!

It's fascinating that *Messiah* should once again turn to the prophets of the Old Testament for words to describe the ministry of Jesus, rather than to the narratives of the Gospels. But the intention seems to be to tie the event to the expectation—to show that Jesus truly was the Messiah because he precisely fulfilled the expectations of the prophets. That wasn't, of course, how the people of Israel at the time saw it. Their expectation was of a conquering king, a successor to David, a liberator and saviour who would restore once again true kingship to Israel. And, of course, they could find those ideas, too, in the prophets.

But there was another, more subtle picture of the Messiah in the Jewish scriptures, a Messiah who was a Shepherd-King, a bringer not of wars of revenge but of a reign of peace. Perhaps we always look for what we hope to see—as we say, 'the wish is father to the thought'. Whatever the reason, the Messiah as a prince of peace was neither expected nor, when he came, accepted.

This section of *Messiah* is itself a kind of peaceful interlude, mirroring in its words and music the most beautiful of lives. Yet it is a vital 'interlude', because it is the life of Jesus on earth that makes his death so poignant, and his resurrection such a source of eternal hope.

13

The king who speaks peace

Rejoice greatly, O daughter of Zion; shout, O daughter of Jerusalem: behold, thy King cometh unto thee: he is the righteous Saviour; and he shall speak peace unto the heathen.

Zechariah 9:9–10

There is a kind of peace that comes from compromise, but true and lasting peace can only come when the elements that make for war have been completely removed.

The picture here is of the women of a city going out to greet the king. They would have been singing psalms of praise mingled with shouts of triumph, and perhaps carrying palm branches or garlands. This is either a newly-crowned king, or a king returning from victory over their enemies.

If you read the passage in Zechariah in full, it is impossible not to think of Jesus entering Jerusalem on Palm Sunday, 'gentle and riding on a donkey', but the key word is probably 'Saviour'. In its context, this is a prophecy of Zion's king driving out the oppressor and re-establishing his rule over the whole of the Holy Land (see Zechariah 9:3–10).

However, in *Messiah* it has a different purpose, and that is to introduce the ministry of Jesus, who came to earth in the lowliest possible circumstances—born in a stable, laid in a manger—but bearing the name 'Jesus', 'for he shall save his people from their sins'.

When I was a child we used to sing a chorus in Sunday school—a song I haven't heard for forty years or more. It went like this:

He did not come to judge the world,
He did not come to blame;
He did not only come to seek
It was to save he came.
And when we call him Saviour
And when we call him Saviour
And when we call him Saviour, then
We call him by his name.

Sometimes the simplest words express the most profound truths. Those certainly do. They echo the words of John 3:17: 'For God did not send the Son into the world to condemn the world, but in order that the world might be saved through him'. The primary purpose of God in sending Jesus into the world was the world's salvation, and so 'Saviour' is his primary and proper title.

And he is the 'righteous Saviour'—that's to say, he comes to do what is right, to do what God requires. He will save his people from their sins, but he will do it without compromising the righteousness and justice of God. There will be no cheap grace, no fudged judgment. When Jesus saves us, he saves us from sin into 'righteousness', which is to say he saves us from something, for something. And the 'something' for which he saves us is God's will and purpose.

'He shall speak peace unto the heathen.' The 'heathen'—the 'nations', the Gentiles—will also hear the message of peace from the Messiah. This, too, will not be a fudged or compromised peace. 'He will cut off the chariot from Ephraim and the war horse from Jerusalem; and the battle bow shall be cut off... his dominion shall be from sea to sea, and from the River to the ends of the earth'. There will be universal disarmament under the supervision of this conquering Saviour, a genuine 'decommissioning of weapons', and peace will prevail wherever he rules.

The angels at Bethlehem sang a message of 'peace on earth', just as Isaiah had foretold that the child to be born would be the 'Prince of Peace'. In the last analysis, the only true peace is that which comes when a greater power has taken away the instruments of war and broken down the barriers which separate people from each other. That was how the early Christians saw the ministry of the Saviour Jesus: 'For he is our peace; in his flesh he has made both groups into one and has broken down the dividing wall, that is, the hostility between us. He has abolished the law with its commandments and ordinances, that he might create in himself one new humanity in place of the two, thus making peace, and might reconcile both groups to God in one body through the cross, thus putting to death that hostility through it' (Ephesians 2:14–16).

Jesus Christ is the Prince of Peace. Rejoice, O daughter of Zion!

In one important sense, the 'peace of Christ' is the peace of conquest, because at its heart is the defeat of sin and death through his cross and resurrection. But it is at the same time a tender peace, because it is not forced on people, but offered as a gift, to be accepted or rejected.

14

A time for healing

Then shall the eyes of the blind be opened, and the ears of the deaf unstopped. Then shall the lame man leap as an hart, and the tongue of the dumb shall sing.

Isaiah 35:5–6

To be healed, to be 'made whole' is much more than simply having something that was wrong put right. It is to be restored to 'wholeness', to be what God intends us to be.

The Gospels tell us that the first public words of Jesus after his baptism were from the book of Isaiah. He stood up in the synagogue in Nazareth, his home town, and read out these words: 'The Spirit of the Lord is upon me, because he has anointed me to bring good news to the poor. He has sent me to proclaim release to the captives and recovery of sight to the blind, to let the oppressed go free, to proclaim the year of the Lord's favour.' Then he handed back the book and told the startled congregation, 'Today this scripture has been fulfilled in your hearing.'

It was, of course, an astonishing claim, for these words from Isaiah (61:1–2) relate to the promise of blessing through the Messiah. He would set the people free, lift up the heads of the poor, rescue captives and slaves from their chains and release the oppressed. Indeed, as the words of this recitative tell us, he would do more than that: he would give sight to the blind, hearing to the deaf, speech to the dumb and mobility to the lame.

In fact, Jesus did not perform such miracles in Nazareth, and the people there ended up by turning on him and would have killed him. Yet the rest of his short ministry on earth was marked by precisely these 'signs'. He gave sight to the blind. He gave speech to the dumb and hearing to the deaf. He told the paralysed man to pick up his bed and walk. He set people free from those things that oppressed them, shut them in, cut them off from their friends and family.

Sadly, when people read the Gospels they tend either to see that Jesus taught the kingdom of God, calling for a new kind of society on principles of righteousness and justice; or that he healed and restored wounded individuals. This leads to the notion that there are two competing gospels, one a message that society can be changed and renewed through the message of Jesus, and the other that individuals can be made whole by him.

In fact, of course, both are true, and both are part of the messianic vision. Both are in the message of the Jewish prophets and both are in the pages of the Gospel writings—right there in the 'core' material. Unlike us, Jesus seemed to hold both in an easy but fruitful tension. He called for justice and compassion for the whole people, and he touched individuals with his healing power. He came, as the prayer says, to 'heal both men and nations'—communities and individuals.

In the words we are thinking of here, each of the physical handicaps that can cut people off from others is identified: being blind, deaf, dumb or unable to walk. The promise is that each of them will be healed by the Messiah when he comes. The blind will see, the deaf hear, the dumb not just speak but sing, and the lame not just walk but 'leap as an hart'. No longer will they feel isolated. Their healing will restore them to life as God intended it to be for them. They have suffered enough, and now they will be lifted up. That is the promise. And, in the ministry of Jesus, the promise was fulfilled. These were signs of the Messiah, and the Messiah offered the signs.

A REFLECTION

Each of us needs to be made whole, because without the grace and love of God we are incomplete. As Jesus saw it, there is a blindness worse than the loss of eyesight, and that is not to be able to 'see' spiritual truths. Some who have speech can't sing for joy. Some who can hear human speech are deaf to the voice of God. For each, the Messiah brings his healing.

15

The gentle shepherd

He shall feed his flock like a shepherd: and he shall gather the lambs with his arm, and carry them in his bosom, and gently lead those that are with young.

Isaiah 40:11

Great strength and great gentleness are not mutually exclusive. Sometimes it requires more courage to be gentle than to be tough.

There was a time when no child's bedroom was complete without a picture of Jesus the Good Shepherd. He was usually seated with a lamb in his arms, and surrounded by remarkably north European looking children! And many children were taught that lovely bed-time prayer, 'Jesus tender Shepherd, hear me, Bless your little lamb tonight...' So the image of Jesus as a shepherd is familiar, even to people who have never seen a shepherd in their lives.

While that image of Jesus as the Good Shepherd is a beautiful and helpful one, it falls some way short of the full meaning of this powerful metaphor. In the history of the Jews, the Shepherd-King was a deeply significant symbol. Good kings cared for their people in the way that shepherds cared for their flocks—and that was by leading them well, keeping them safe, providing for their material needs and, if necessary, laying down their own lives to defend them. You can find all of those ideas in the famous 'Shepherd Psalm', the twenty-third.

The words of this aria are taken from a passage in Isaiah where the prophet is offering exactly such a picture. Indeed, these words of tender care come after a reminder of God's awesome power and strength: 'See, the Lord God comes with might, and his arm rules for him; his reward is with him, and his recompense before him'. It was precisely because God is a God of infinite power and might that he could fulfil the role of shepherd to his people.

After all, to be a shepherd in the ancient world was no job for a weakling. It involved long hours out on the hills, exposed to all weather and to perils from wild animals and brigands. At night, the shepherd lay across the entrance to the sheep fold, his own body forming a barrier against predators, whether human or animal. It was by no means uncommon for a shepherd to give his life for his sheep. The most famous shepherd in the history of Israel was, of course, David, who was brought from the hills to be anointed as the future king—'ruddy', as the Bible tells us, and 'handsome'—what we might call a 'rough diamond'.

So the Messiah stands before his people as a strong but tender shepherd, powerful in opposing all that is evil but gentle with the weak, the bruised, the lost. It is such a Shepherd that we need— one who has power over evil, but understands our weaknesses and failures; one who risks his life for the lost sheep.

In his earthly ministry Jesus seemed to work to this principle. He was hard—almost ruthless, one feels—with hypocrites and the self-righteous, but infinitely gentle with failures, whether their failure was physical or moral. He looked with compassion on the ulcerated limbs of the leper, and healed him. He wept at the tomb of Lazarus, and brought him back to his grieving sisters. He forgave the woman taken in adultery and scornfully dismissed her accusers. Like a shepherd, he knew which of his charges needed to be carried near his heart, which needed feeding, which were in danger of straying from the path. And, like a shepherd, he 'laid down his life for the sheep'.

A REFLECTION

It should not surprise me that when I am feeling able to look after myself, God often speaks words of warning and challenge. But when I am feeling lost and helpless, he takes me in his arms. This is the Shepherd heart of God.

16

The way to rest

Come unto him, all ye that labour, come unto him, that are heavy laden, and he will give you rest. Take his yoke upon you, and learn of him; for he is meek and lowly of heart: and ye shall find rest unto your souls.

Matthew 11:28–29

There is no point in placing our burdens on those who are unwilling or unable to carry them. The perfect burden-bearer is willing and able, but can only bear what we are prepared to transfer.

Messiah takes the liberty here of transposing these words of Jesus from the first person ('Come unto me...') to the third ('Come unto him...'), but the invitation remains the same. Jesus, during his earthly ministry, spent a great deal of his time bearing other people's burdens. He consoled the sad, healed the sick, touched the outcasts, fed the hungry crowds, saved a wedding feast from disaster when the wine ran out. He has been called 'the Man for others', and that's a very fair description of his approach. No one who turned to him was sent away empty. No one who asked for his help was told he was too busy, or had more important things to do.

So when Jesus said to the people of his day, 'Come unto me, you that labour and are heavy laden', it was an invitation full of hope. They had seen what he could do, and he was now offering that same strength, support and help to those who needed it most. It was not an invitation to those who found life easy, but to those who found it very hard. In that sense, it was selective. But in the time of Jesus there were many people who lived, by present-day Western standards at least, in abject poverty and hunger. His concern for the poor is evident all through the Gospels. But a further burden on the people of his time was the 'yoke' of legalistic religion. The rabbis spoke of 'the yoke of the Law' which God's people should be proud to carry. But for the poor and oppressed, especially, the Law itself was sometimes the last straw that broke the camel's back. So in every way this offer was to those who lived under crushing burdens of outward poverty or inward care. 'Come unto me...'

Do his words have anything to say to us, most of whom do not live in abject poverty or face crushing demands on us day by day? The first thing to say is that they emphatically do speak with power and hope to those, today as in every age, who are poor, or trapped in circumstances which make life a crushing burden. There are those who care for an elderly loved one, or a severely handicapped son or daughter, for instance. But there are also those whose burdens are less physical, but no less exhausting— those struggling with instincts and inner drives that they find hard to control, those living in loveless and even violent relationships from which there seems no escape, those longing to be rid of sins that threaten to destroy them. And there are some, now as then, for whom religion itself, sadly, is a heavy load to bear. These are all grievous burdens, which make their bearers feel 'heavy laden'.

So how can Jesus Christ relieve the strain? In what sense can he, who is no longer with us in the flesh, be a 'burden bearer'? The answer is in that old word 'yoke'. A yoke linked two beasts of burden, which in normal circumstances would mean that the load was halved for each of them. I say 'in normal circumstances', because sometimes the owner would partner a very young or inexperienced ox with an older and stronger one. Then the burden was not shared equally—the stronger animal bore more than half the burden, while the weaker one drew strength from its partner. That is the model of Christ's yoke. The burden is shared, but our 'partner' bears more than half of it. The 'strong Son of God' holds up the weak children of Man.

The ox had to bow its head and accept the wooden yoke that harnessed it not only to the load but to the other ox who would share it. For us, taking a 'yoke' involves humility, in other words— a recognition that this load could not be borne alone. It's still true that some of us would rather bear our private burdens, however 'heavy laden' we are, than humbly turn to Christ for help. Yet the invitation remains, however obstinately we may have refused it in the past. 'Come unto me, ye that labour and are heavy laden, and I will give you rest.'

A REFLECTION

In Matthew's Gospel this lovely invitation of Jesus follows two important sayings. The first is that the Father hides the deepest truths from the wise and learned and reveals them to little children (v. 25). The second is that all things have been committed to Jesus by the Father (v. 27). Then this invitation follows, as though its sheer simplicity will attract those who have a burden, and the power and strength of the Father will be available to help them to bear it.

17

The light burden

His yoke is easy, and his burthen is light.

Matthew 11:30

Sometimes a quite trivial thing becomes a huge burden; sometimes a heavy responsibility can be lightly borne. It's not the size of the load that makes the difference, but how we see it.

There was a pop song back in the 1970s which talked about bearing a load on a long journey—a person who had to be carried. However, as the refrain explained, 'He ain't heavy, he's my brother!' I thought of that song the other day as I watched a young mother carrying a bonny baby up a steep stairway. I'm sure she would never have thought of her child as a tiresome burden. In other words, even heavy loads can be acceptable, indeed, can be joyfully carried. It all depends what it is!

I think that's what lies behind this deceptively simple saying of Jesus. 'My yoke', he said, 'is light, my burden easy'. This doesn't mean that putting on the yoke of Jesus involves lesser demands on us than, say, the Law of Moses, or that being his disciple is a bed of roses compared with ordinary life. After all, he makes it plain to his disciples that to follow him involves 'taking up the cross daily', 'denying yourself', being prepared to 'lose your life for his sake' (see Matthew 16:24, 25).

Yet it is 'light'. The Greek word used in the Gospel usually means 'kind', and it probably refers back here to Jesus' words just before: 'Take my yoke upon you, and learn of me: for I am meek and lowly in heart'. The yoke of Jesus is 'light' or 'kind' because he is 'meek and lowly'—that is, gentle and humble. He would not load us with cruel or unnecessary burdens, because that would be against his nature.

And, of course, as we have seen, the burden is to be shared, not carried on our own. The 'yoke' placed on the disciple is also placed on Jesus. We are not left to carry our burdens unaided. That is another reason why the yoke is 'light'—in the old saying, 'a burden shared is a burden halved'. Jesus does place responsibilities on us. Of course he does. But he then offers to share them with us, if we 'come to him'.

That, of course, is the crux of the matter. The burden we carry at his command was never meant to be a solo task! Yet often we are reluctant to 'come to him' for help with it, as though that would in some way be an admission of personal failure. Many of us know this feeling from our daily work. Having been given a task to do, we're reluctant to seek advice or help with it because that might call our competence into question. So instead we either do it badly or worry and agonize over it, when all the while there is help at hand which we are refusing to accept.

'Come to me,' says Jesus, 'with your burden.' It's a marvellous invitation, made even better by his assurance that, if we do, his burden on us is light, his yoke is easy and kind.

A REFLECTION

St Paul told the Corinthian Christians that God would not allow them to be tested beyond what they could bear, but would always provide a 'way out' (1 Corinthians 10:13). Often, and for many of us, that 'way out' will be the shared yoke of Jesus Christ, who comes alongside to help us bear our burdens.

THE SUFFERING MESSIAH

The pastoral interlude is over. The three years of the ministry of Jesus are drawing to their close. As the Messiah he has walked the lanes of Galilee and the streets of Jerusalem speaking words of wisdom and challenge and love. He has stopped by the roadside to heal the sick and restore sight to the blind. He has joined the fishermen and multiplied their catch of fish. He has calmed the fearful storm on the lake and the more elusive storm of fear in their hearts. He has fed the crowds with bread and fish. As the common people said of him, 'He has done everything well' (Mark 7:37).

And this ministry of love, forgiveness, healing and renewal has led some to recognize that Jesus of Nazareth is indeed the Messiah, the promised Saviour of his people. Indeed, there is at this point a widespread hope that this charismatic rabbi will lead the people into a new era of freedom and independence. They know the prophecies of their scriptures and expect God one day to vindicate his chosen people. Perhaps, they think, that moment has come.

But in fact they have not read the scriptures correctly. The deliverer who was to come would not necessarily be a warrior king like David. If Second Isaiah is right, he would be a 'Suffering Servant of the Lord', who would save his people not by conquest but by self-sacrifice. Jesus had always included in his teaching a warning as well as a promise. The 'Son of man'—the way he usually referred to himself—had not come to be served but to serve, and to 'give his life a ransom for many' (Mark 10:45). Now, as Jesus made his way for the last time towards the Holy City of Jerusalem, they were to discover exactly what that would mean— for him, and for them.

18

The burden bearer

Behold the Lamb of God, that taketh away the sin of the world.

John 1:29

There is one burden that only the Son of God can bear, and that is the burden which we have placed on ourselves, the sheer weight of moral failure.

I remember reading these words from John's Gospel—for the first time, I think, consciously—in the chapel of an RAF station during my National Service. Like many people brought up in a church-going home, I was feeling very rebellious against the faith of my parents. But I did like singing, and enrolling in the chapel choir got you off some pretty unpleasant kitchen duties. So here I was, learning to sing these words set to music by Merbecke: 'Behold the Lamb of God, that taketh away the sin of the world.'

I knew they referred to Jesus, of course, but as they sank into my consciousness it was the sheer enormity of the claim that struck me. 'The sin of the world'! That was something of cosmic dimensions, embracing not just my sins and faults (which, as an eighteen-year-old, I thought were no concern of anybody else, least of all God), but all the huge injustices, violence, evil and depravity that was at work in the world (which, as a highly political animal, were of great concern to me). How could one man, even a man like Jesus, be seen as the 'taker away' of the sin of the world?

It was a couple of years before I began really to grasp the answer to that question, but it was these words at that moment that set me on a journey of exploration that ended in what I can only call a truly 'life-changing' experience.

The words were spoken by John the Baptist to some of his own disciples. He directed their attention away from himself to Jesus, the one who came after John but, in the Baptist's own words, surpassed him. Jesus, they must understand, was the one who would 'take away the sin of the world'—sin which John had been denouncing in no uncertain terms, and calling on people to repent of. John could, and did, wash away the outward signs of sin through baptism with water, but he knew that only Jesus could actually take it away.

So these words, spoken at the very start of the ministry of Jesus, in fact make a fitting introduction to the consideration of the death of Jesus, which brought that earthly ministry to an end. They encapsulate its meaning. The death of Jesus on the cross was not simply the sad and sickening end to a lovely life. It was not only one of the greatest miscarriages of justice in history—probably the greatest. It was not only a marvellous example of pain and abuse nobly and bravely borne. It was all of those things, of course, but these words tell us that it was more, much more.

Jesus was the 'Lamb of God'. That's not a title that immediately makes much sense to a modern Western person, who may see lambs playing in the fields in the spring but in other respects considers them only as a source of food. For the Jews the lamb had a very special role. It was central to the greatest act of deliverance in their history—indeed, the act that defined their very nationhood and shaped from that moment their religion and their destiny. At the Passover meal, which the Jews ate 'in haste' as they prepared to escape from slavery in Egypt a thousand years before Christ, it was a lamb, taken from the flock and slain, that provided both meat to eat and blood to daub on the door-posts. The meat would strengthen them for the journey. The blood would guarantee that the angel of death, as it went through the land of Egypt on its dreadful mission of judgment on the families of the land, would 'pass over' the homes of the Hebrews.

After that, lambs and goats were to be part of the complex rituals of the tabernacle and eventually the temple, where the death of an innocent animal would, they understood, 'atone' for the sins of the people. The lamb was not just food, in other words, but sacrifice.

And Jesus was 'the Lamb of God'. That was John's cryptic but powerful endorsement of the new prophet. He would not just preach against sin, or wash away its outward stains. He would, in himself, 'take it away'. Indeed, in that RAF chapel long ago I could also read the words in Latin: 'qui tollet peccata mundi'—who 'bears as a burden' the sins of the world. The Greek word used in the Gospel has a similar weight to it—airo is 'to lift, take up, bear off something'. This was no light load, but the heaviest burden in the whole history of the creation. Jesus, the Son of God, took upon himself the weight and burden of the world's sin—individual and corporate, personal and structural... and carried it away.

So it is wholly fitting that Messiah introduces the story of our redemption through Jesus with these profound and vivid words. Sacrifice, as a religious principle, isn't a congenial one to modern thinking, and even less do we relish the idea of animals being slaughtered as atonement for human sin. Yet somewhere in this concept is the heart of a great truth, which we ignore at our peril. Sin is real and serious, and there is a price to pay for it. That price, in the ancient world, was a life sacrificed. John the Baptist pointed to Jesus and said that there was the life that was to be sacrificed, and he might have added, 'And after that there will be no more sacrifice for sin, for none will be needed.' The burden Jesus carried to the cross was nothing less than the sin of the world, but the good news is that it was all of it.

A REFLECTION

When Christian, in Bunyan's Pilgrim's Progress, *reached the foot of the cross, he found that the burden on his back that had weighed him down all through his journey, was taken away. That is the consequence of Jesus, the 'Lamb of God', taking upon himself the sin of the world. It's not simply an academic exercise. To be forgiven, to have sin 'taken away', really makes a difference.*

19

The rejected saviour

He was despised and rejected of men; a man of sorrows, and acquainted with grief. He gave his back to the smiters, and his cheeks to them that plucked off the hair: He hid not his face from shame and spitting.

Isaiah 53:3; 50:6

The crucifixion was in itself a barbaric act. But the Messiah had to endure not only the physical agony, but also abuse and scorn from the very people he had come to save.

The Gospels are content for the most part simply to relate the awful events of the betrayal, trial, torture and crucifixion of Jesus, almost as though the writers could not bear to add anything by way of comment or explanation. 'This is what happened,' they seem to say. 'These are the facts as we have received them. Make of them what you will. They are too terrible to need any embellishment and too compelling to need any explanation.'

So once again *Messiah* turns to the prophecies of the Hebrew scriptures, to create in vivid words and poignant music the background to this awful story. Handel and Jennens simply assume that we know the facts. They want us to understand their meaning.

So we have this picture of the Suffering Servant of the Lord. It's possible Isaiah saw himself in that role, or perhaps, one day, the whole people of Israel. But Christians will agree with the evangelist Philip who assured the Ethiopian eunuch that the prophet spoke about 'Jesus' (see Acts 8:34, 35). Indeed, the Gospel accounts of the crucifixion read like a series of tableaux depicting the sorrows of the Servant.

He was rejected. That was probably the cruellest blow of all. As John's Gospel puts it, 'He came to what was his own, and his own people did not accept him' (1:11). He was Israel's Saviour, sent to rescue 'the lost sheep of the house of Israel', but in the end the sheep rejected the Shepherd.

The Gospel stories of the crucifixion don't spare the people. 'His blood be on us and on our children'... 'He saved others; he cannot save himself'... 'He is the king of Israel; let him come down from the cross now, and we will believe in him.' It was not simply that the people acquiesced in his death, though that would have been bad enough. They are seen to be part of the torture. The one who had come to be their saviour ended up as a despised and rejected failure, to be abused and ridiculed.

He was 'a man of sorrows'—a strange phrase, yet very profound. Jesus was not a 'sorrowful man', but a 'man of sorrows', which is rather different. He was a man who experienced sorrows. Indeed, it is hard to think of any sorrow which is common to human experience which he did not experience in his short life, only excepting the experience of committing sin. He knew poverty and homelessness; his father, Joseph, died, probably while Jesus was still growing up; he was hungry and tired at times; he knew spiritual isolation ('My God, my God, why have you forsaken me?'); he was betrayed by a colleague and denied by a friend; he was the victim of blatant injustice and, at the end, suffered ridicule, torture and one of the most painful deaths ever devised by the warped mind of humanity. 'Man of Sorrows' seems a very good title for him.

Yet all of those experiences are part of his being a complete Saviour. As the letter to the Hebrews says, 'For we do not have a high priest who is unable to sympathize with our weaknesses, but we have one who in every respect has been tested as we are, yet without sin' (Hebrews 4:15). No suffering creature can shake a fist at God and say, 'You don't understand what I'm going through'. In his Son, God has encountered the pain of human sorrow, and drunk the cup to its bitter dregs.

The words from Isaiah 50—'He gave his back to the smiters, and his cheeks to them that plucked off the hair...'—are often omitted from performances of *Messiah*, but they portray vividly the complete loss of dignity involved in the ritual of crucifixion. The mocking of the soldiers and their insults and spitting may seem little compared to the pain of the crucifixion itself, but the sheer degradation of the victim is caught in these words. Yet, for the sake of those he came to save, the Servant of the Lord did not hide his face from shame. There is an awful, divine dignity about Jesus, even when he was at the mercy of his captors. If this was the price of redemption, then the Suffering Servant would pay it.

'Man of Sorrows' is a title which Jesus bore not as an insult but as a crown because the 'sorrows' that he bore were the pains and evil and sadness of the human race, the very people he had come to save.

20

Broken for me

Surely, surely he hath borne our griefs, and carried our
sorrows: he was wounded for our transgressions, he was
bruised for our iniquities: the chastisement of our peace was
upon him; and with his stripes we are healed.

Isaiah 53:4–5

Suffering can be personal and private, or collective and public. The suffering of Jesus seems to have combined every element: it was personal but public, individual but collective. He died himself, but his death was entirely for others.

The word 'surely', repeated so tellingly in the opening bars of this chorus, sets the scene. We have been introduced to the Suffering Servant of the Lord, 'despised and rejected', the 'man of sorrows'. But now we are given the reason for it: 'surely he hath borne our griefs'. This is its reason, its meaning, its purpose. This was no blind tragedy, but a working out of the sure purposes of God.

If 'surely' introduces the idea, capturing a sense of purpose, then the other key word must be 'for'. The brief preposition gives meaning to every sentence. He has borne our griefs for us, he has carried sorrows for us; for our transgressions he was wounded, for our iniquities he was bruised. 'The chastisement of our peace'—that's to say, the punishment that brings us peace—was carried by him, not by us. And our healing comes through his 'stripes': his wounds heal us.

The whole passage speaks of sacrifice, not now the offering for sin, but the sacrifice made for our good. Just as there was a price for forgiveness, so there is a price for wholeness. There is no 'cheap grace', in Bonhoeffer's memorable phrase. It costs something to heal the wounds of bruised humanity, to bear its sorrows and earn its peace. Healing is wholeness, being made whole, and in a mysterious way the healing of the human race flows from the offering of the life of Jesus. 'His wounds heal us.'

St Peter quotes some of these words (1 Peter 2:24) and applies them directly to the sacrifice of Jesus on the cross. 'He himself bore our sins in his body on the cross, so that, free from sin, we might live for righteousness; by his wounds you have been healed.' The apostle sees the cross both as the forgiveness of sin and the source of true inner healing—that wholeness which is God's will for all his people. Because Jesus died for sin, we can be forgiven. Because Jesus suffered, human suffering can be healed. This is not so much a doctrine of substitution as of liberation. The death of Jesus, the obedient servant of the Father, releases us from the results of human disobedience. We are not simply spared the penalty for our sins, but released from their consequences.

All through the history of the Church theologians have argued as to precisely how this could be brought about. Doctrines and theories of the 'atonement' have been debated and even fought over. Even today, there are Christians who will insist that the benefits and blessings of the death of Jesus must be appropriated in this or that manner, in accordance with a particular way of understanding the cross.

To be honest, I can't see in the New Testament any one all-embracing theory of atonement. What I can find is half a dozen different ways of understanding what is, essentially, a 'mystery'. I am content, for myself, to say that whatever Jesus did when he died on the cross, he did it for us, not for himself. In fact, like St Paul, I would like to go a bit further than that. He spoke of the 'Son of God, who loved me, and gave himself for me' (Galatians 2:20). And the emphasis, as he wrote the words, is on the personal pronoun: he loved *me*, and gave himself for *me*. Whatever Jesus did on that barren hill outside Jerusalem two thousand years ago, he did it for me, so that I could be healed, made whole, brought back as an obedient child to his Father.

A REFLECTION

The 'Man of Sorrows' was also the 'Man for Others'. There is something indescribably splendid about a life lived so conspicuously for the good of other people, and a death offered so totally for the forgiveness and healing of those who need it. Christ couldn't die for his own sins, because he hadn't any, so he died for those who needed it, instead.

21

Harassed and helpless

All we like sheep have gone astray; we have turned every one to his own way; and the Lord hath laid on him the iniquity of us all.

Isaiah 53:6

Human sin is often a mixture of stupidity, wilfulness and the unresisted influence of others. That doesn't make it less serious. Unlike sheep, human beings are responsible for their own actions.

'Sheep' seem to figure widely in *Messiah*, and usually in a complimentary way. Sheep are protected and cared for by the shepherd-king. Sheep are led along good paths and the little lambs are carried in his arms. But here is another, contrasting picture of sheep, one with which country people are very familiar. Sheep are, to put it bluntly, stupid.

My wife and I spend a lot of time in Wales, often driving along narrow country lanes closed in by high hedges. Along such roads there is a major hazard: wandering sheep, usually in the plural. As the car approaches they look up. The sight and the noise is obviously frightening, so they decide to move out of the way. But they don't do the obvious, which would be to go sideways, as it were, up the bank into the hedge. That's what a rabbit would do, or a stoat, or a squirrel. But not a sheep, because to exit up the bank would require an infinitesimal bit of lateral thinking, and sheep aren't capable of that. So they simply turn and run away in front of the car down the road. If the car gets near, they go faster. If it stops, they might well do the same. Unless someone—the driver or a passer-by or the farmer—steers them off the road into a gateway or gap in the bank, they will go on running like that all day.

When Matthew's Gospel calls sheep 'harassed and helpless' it is saying no more than the observable truth. They wander about in confusion unless firmly led or forcefully directed. They are helpless because even in the basic matter of survival they are unable to look after themselves. So it's not much of a compliment to people to be told that we are like sheep.

So, 'All we like sheep have gone astray'—or, as the old *Book of Common Prayer* says, 'We have strayed from thy ways like lost sheep'. Or, in the saying of Matthew 9:36 already quoted, 'the crowds... were harassed and helpless, like sheep without a shepherd'. People without God, people living as though God doesn't exist, people living in disregard of his law and purposes, are sheep-like.

Handel's music seems to imply that the sheep are silly rather than downright evil. The words are set to a dance-like melody. But where people are concerned it is much more serious than that. The 'sheep' in question, who are people like us, are 'lost' not because of bad luck or the shepherd's incompetence, but of their own choice: 'We have turned every one to his own way'. Human 'sheep' may well be silly, stupid even, but we are not innocent. We have chosen to go our own way, not the shepherd's. It is a dangerous choice to make.

There is another characteristic of sheep that is relevant here. Sheep seldom operate on their own. They wander about in flocks, and tend to imitate each other's behaviour. If the first sheep jumps over an obstacle which is subsequently removed, the rest of the sheep, in blind imitation, will jump over a non-existent object. Sheep, in other words, tend not to think for themselves, but to do what all the other sheep are doing.

Obviously these words of Isaiah refer to human beings. It is 'we', all of us, who have 'gone astray'. If the last chorus dealt with the meaning of the cross of Jesus, then this one offers a cause for it. People have gone astray. People have turned their backs on God. People have chosen to disobey his laws. They have not done these things through ignorance or even stupidity, but by deliberate choice. They have, very often, taken more notice of what the 'crowd' thinks than of what God commands.

But the Good Shepherd is not content to leave things like that. The sheep are lost, so the Shepherd comes seeking them: 'The Son of Man has come to seek and to save what was lost'. Jesus, the Messiah, is the good shepherd who goes out in search of the lost sheep and will not relent until he finds it.

But these words go further than that. 'The Lord has laid on him the iniquity of us all.' It will cost something to bring back the lost sheep. Indeed, it will cost the Shepherd his life. The failure and sin and sheer wilfulness of his human 'sheep' will be 'laid on' Jesus. As he himself said, 'The good shepherd lays down his life for his sheep'.

We are lost sheep, but it is the 'Lamb of God' who comes to rescue us! By our own choice we have gone dancing off, deserting the Shepherd's chosen paths, yet in his love he still comes searching for us—and is prepared to give his life for the sheep. The Servant of the Lord is the Shepherd of the sheep, and their Saviour.

22

Misunderstood

*All they that see him laugh him to scorn: they shoot out
their lips, and shake their heads, saying, He trusted in God
that he would deliver him: let him deliver him, if he delight
in him.*

Psalm 22:7–8 (BCP)

**There is no experience as bitter as misplaced trust, so to go on trust-
ing someone when all the evidence is against it is the ultimate test
of faith.**

People sometimes speak of the 'dereliction' of Christ on the
cross—his utter abandonment, first of all by friends and supporters, and then, it seemed, for one dark hour, even by his heavenly
Father. That sense of dereliction, of being left alone to face the
horror of evil, must have been as painful as the nails in his hands
and feet.

There were heady moments on Palm Sunday, when crowds of
cheering Galileans ushered him into the city. Yet within five days
everything changed. Judas Iscariot—'one of the Twelve'—
betrayed him to the authorities. His friend Peter denied to a teas-
ing audience that he had ever known him. The abandonment
must have seemed cruelly abrupt. Suddenly, when he needed
them most, he had no friends.

In Gethsemane Jesus wrestled with his despair. His heart was
'deeply grieved, even to death'. Must he drink this cup? Was there
no other way? The words seemed to be wrung from him: 'yet, not
my will but yours be done'. It was a touching note of Luke's to
record that at that moment 'an angel from heaven appeared to
him and gave him strength' (Luke 22:43).

The sacrifice was his, and his alone. Though it was made to fulfil his Father's will, it was by his own free decision that the Saviour
made it, so that by the obedience of the Son of Man the disobedient 'sons of men' could be redeemed (see Romans 5:19). But it was
a lonely decision that he had to make, and it was alone that he
went to Golgotha.

It was not simply that no one seemed to stand by him—always
excepting, of course, those faithful women who followed and

stood at a distance to watch the awful event. It was that no one understood—indeed, no one could understand. The disciples were baffled that the one who had given sight to the blind and even life to the dead should now submit himself to crucifixion at the hands of evil men. The crowds were sarcastic: 'He saved others, but he can't save himself.' His enemies, the religious leaders and their allies, were openly scornful, fulfilling the prophetic words of this Psalm, which speaks of the faithful servant of the Lord becoming an object of public ridicule, abandoned in his moment of need by the God he had faithfully served.

The Psalm opens with the agonized question that was wrung from the lips of Jesus as he died: 'My God, my God, why have you forsaken me?' It would seem that the words of this Psalm were with him all through that evil day of suffering. But if they were, then the answer to the question was also in his mind: 'For he [the Lord] did not despise or abhor the affliction of the afflicted; he did not hide his face from me, but heard when I cried to him' (Psalm 22:24).

Dereliction—abandonment by those we have trusted—is a terrible experience. I remember an uncle of mine who was ruined by a disloyal business partner. The loss of money was painful, but it was the thought of betrayal by one he had trusted implicitly that really hurt, and, we felt, led to his death. The onlookers at the crucifixion were taunting Jesus with the failure of the God in whom he had trusted. Jesus knew, and had been twice re-assured of the fact during his ministry, that the Father called him 'My Son, the one in whom I am well pleased'. Now those very words were being thrown into his face. Why wouldn't the Father now act to deliver his Son, 'if he delight in him'?

The answer, of course, was that to have rescued Jesus from the cross would have made his sacrifice pointless. All that Jesus had gone through would have been thrown away. When the crowd said, 'He saved others, himself he cannot save' they spoke the truth, without knowing it. In order to save others—in order to save us—he could not save himself. It was only through the freely offered life of the Son of God that those erring 'sons of men' could be saved. It was not God's 'wrath' or 'judgment' that bound Jesus to the cross, but his love. And it was not some misguided sense of martyrdom that made Jesus accept the cross, but that same love. Love must be freely offered: and love is often cruelly misunderstood as weakness.

The cross is a mystery, probably the most profound mystery in the whole of creation. And part of the mystery is encapsulated in these words of scorn addressed to the lone figure on the hill. God did delight in his Son, but to have 'delivered' him would have been to make all that Jesus had been through meaningless.

A REFLECTION

In my moments of self-pity at the way I feel I have been misunderstood or let down by friends, may I reflect on the mystery of the Son of God accepting ridicule, scorn and abuse from the very people he was dying to save.

23

The loneliness of the cross

Thy rebuke hath broken his heart; he is full of heaviness: he looked for some to have pity on him, but there was no man, neither found he any to comfort him.

Psalm 69:21 (BCP) *v. 20 elsewhere*

Messiah opens with a promise of comfort. But for the one God had appointed to bring the comfort, there was no comfort at all.

I remember a speaker in a youth meeting probably forty years ago saying that 'Jesus died a real death for real sins'. I can also remember the impact it had on me. Though the words seem obvious, I can still recall the shock. I think until then I had rather imagined the crucifixion as a kind of play, acted out between Jesus, his Father and the powers of evil, with the result pre-determined. After all, it ended in resurrection. The thought that Jesus died a 'real' death—the sort of death human convicts might suffer at the hands of an executioner, or that ordinary people might experience in hospital or in their sick room—was almost shocking. This was the Son of God. How could the one through whom the world was created end up like one of his mortal creatures?

But the message of these words, taken from Psalm 69, is of the loneliness of human suffering, a loneliness that Jesus experienced on the cross. The psalmist, possibly writing at a time when Jerusalem had been destroyed by the armies of Nebuchadnezzar at the beginning of the sixth century BC, utters a cry of desperation as much as faith. All through it echoes with the agony of despair: 'rescue me from sinking in the mire; let me be delivered from my enemies and from the deep waters. Do not let the flood sweep over me, or the deep swallow me up, or the Pit close its mouth over me' (Psalm 69:14–15).

And worst of all, he was to face it alone. 'I have become a stranger to my kindred, an alien to my mother's children' (v. 8). He cried to God in desperation, because all human help had abandoned him.

We may ask how relevant these words are to Jesus on the cross. Certainly *Messiah* chooses to emphasize the abandonment of Jesus, rather than his calm and trusting acceptance of the Father's will—it follows Mark's Gospel, in other words, rather than Luke's. But that is only to choose between two absolutely true and relevant insights. Jesus did trust his Father implicitly, and even in the darkest hour of suffering never doubted his purposes. Yet he also experienced a degree of isolation from the Father which opened up the Godhead to something completely new, the pain of mortality. The translation used here (from the *Book of Common Prayer*) implies that it was the Lord's 'rebuke' that had broken his heart, but God was not 'rebuking' his Son. The 'rebuke' (as all other translations make clear) was human—the scorn and reproaches of the crowds, the vicious words of his enemies.

And there was no one to comfort him. That is a stark and bitter truth. His mother stood by the cross, it is true, to be joined at some point by 'the disciple he loved', John. The faithful women stood at a distance. But the scene was filled with hatred and alienation—the indifferent soldiers doing their job, the mocking priests, the scornful crowd. In the centre of this circle of hatred hung the King of love. History can offer no paradox to equal that.

Isaiah had promised centuries before that comfort would come with the arrival of the Messiah. Now he had come, and he was winning 'comfort' for the world on the cross. But for the one who was dying there, there was no comfort at all, except that he was doing the will of his Father.

A REFLECTION

When we are called upon to experience abuse, and especially to bear it alone, we can reflect that the Son of God has been there before us. Like the psalmist, we may feel let down, even abandoned by God. But the Psalm ends not with despair, but with faith. 'The Lord hears the needy and does not despise his captive people. Let heaven and earth praise him!'

24

The Suffering Servant

Behold, and see if there be any sorrow like unto his sorrow.

Lamentations 1:12

He was cut off out of the land of the living: for the transgression of thy people was he stricken.

Isaiah 53:8

'There is joy for all the members in the sorrows of the Head' (F.W. Faber). To suffer on behalf of another is not to suffer pointlessly but positively.

Messiah brings together here two sayings from the Hebrew scriptures which are about suffering and the price of disobedience. The first, from the book of Lamentations, is the sad voice of a stricken city. Jerusalem is in ruins, wrecked by invading armies, and the writer imagines a voice emerging, as it were, from the rubble. 'Behold, and see if there be any sorrow like unto my sorrow, which is done unto me.' It is a cry of sheer grief, but as the context makes clear, it is also a recognition that what has happened is a judgment of God on Jerusalem's past sins and disobedience. The Assyrians may have knocked down the buildings, but it is 'the Lord' who is at work, 'in the day of his fierce anger'. Those are not pleasant ideas for a modern reader of the Bible to accept. Why would a loving God treat even erring children in this appalling way?

The second saying is from the well-known fifty-third chapter of Isaiah, the song of the 'Suffering Servant'. This is a message about a 'Servant of the Lord', a Messiah figure, who will save the people of that same city, Jerusalem, by suffering for them. The language of the passage is not easy and people argue over precisely what the words were meant to convey. But there seems little doubt that the Servant would, as this verse says, 'be stricken for the transgressions of thy people'. That's to say, in some way *his* suffering would release the people from *theirs*—suffering brought upon them by their own 'transgressions', breaches of the law.

Taken together, *Messiah* suggests that these two sayings

provide a picture of the cost of redemption. Applied to Jesus, they invite us to consider the extent of his 'sorrow'. There is no harm at all from time to time in contemplating the appalling suffering which Christ endured. It was so much more than just the physical pain, as we have already seen. There was the rejection by those he had come to save. There was abuse and scorn and the rank injustice of his sentence, a 'miscarriage of justice' if ever there was one.

Isaiah's Suffering Servant was to endure all of those things, too, including being completely misunderstood by the people: 'We accounted him struck down by God' (Isaiah 53:4). He was stricken, of course, but not because of any failure or guilt on his part. He was stricken for their 'iniquities', not his own. And this was 'the Lord's will' (v. 10). We don't need to think in terms of God 'punishing' his Servant instead of the people. That's too crude an idea. Instead, we can think of God sending his Servant to spare the people the consequences of their sins. It was an act of mercy and love, not of retribution. But it certainly involved the 'chosen one', the Servant of the Lord—or, in the case of Jesus, God's own Son—in very real and bitter suffering.

It's usual nowadays to think of the medieval concentration on the physical suffering of Jesus as unhealthy, and perhaps such ideas as being 'hidden in his wounds' and so on do seem rather extreme to us. But it may be we have over-reacted. Could it be that time spent, even once a year, in serious reflection on the cost of what God did for us through his Son would re-awaken our love for him? Our redemption was neither cheap nor easy. The suffering of Jesus, the Lord's perfect 'Suffering Servant', expresses more vividly than anything else the extent of God's love for his erring children.

That leaves the question of desert. Jerusalem came to accept its guilt. They had enjoyed enormous privileges as God's 'chosen people', but they had presumed on them and abused his generosity. What was to come upon the city was no more than they deserved. Yet, according to these words of Isaiah, even the guilty people were to receive mercy. When the Saviour came he would stand with them in their guilt, and in some infinitely mysterious way take it upon himself. Though himself guiltless, he would be 'wounded for our transgression'. Though the Lord's faithful Servant, he would be 'bruised for our iniquities'. We are the ones who have gone astray, like foolish sheep. He is the one on whom 'the Lord has laid the iniquity of us all'.

*It was hard for the Jewish people to accept that their great
Deliverer would achieve the Lord's victory through suffering. That
same paradox is often just as hard for us to understand: 'the
message about the cross is foolishness', said St Paul. Yet in that
apparent contradiction there is a key to true wisdom. Indeed, in
that same passage St Paul calls the crucified Jesus 'the power of
God and the wisdom of God'. In the end we shall discover that life
only makes sense when viewed through the cross.*

THE RISEN MESSIAH

A t this point *Messiah* moves from Good Friday to the events of the first Easter. Typically, the story of the resurrection of Jesus is told almost entirely in the words of the Old Testament prophets rather than the Gospel writers. In that way, we are assured that this was no unexpected sequence of unlikely events, but a messianic plan which God had devised, revealed centuries before to the seers and psalmists of Israel and finally confirmed in the coming of the Messiah Jesus.

After the sombre darkness of suffering and death, both words and music explode into glorious acclamation. The cross, which seemed like defeat, is revealed as the gateway to triumph. The darkness and suffering of Golgotha give way to the bright and shining light of the empty tomb. The eventual enthronement of the risen Jesus at the right hand of the majesty on high is nothing less than the coronation of a triumphant Prince.

So the whole mood changes. If one were tempted to think that *Messiah* had made too much of the doom and gloom of human rebellion and sin, they are now revealed as no more than the backdrop for the splendour of God's saving plan.

The empty tomb

*But thou didst not leave his soul in hell; nor didst thou suffer
thy Holy One to see corruption.*

Psalm 16:10

**In the perspective of eternity, there is nothing unlikely or surpris-
ing about the resurrection of Jesus. If he shared the divine nature,
then it was not feasible that he should remain dead.**

Every now and then Jennens, in compiling the words of *Messiah*,
takes liberties with the text of the King James Bible. This is a particularly glaring example, because he changes the tense of the
verbs from future to past: 'thou wilt not...' to 'thou didst not', and
'neither wilt thou...' to 'nor didst thou'. His reason is simple: that
which the psalmist had placed in the future was now in the past.
What had been dimly foreseen perhaps 900 years earlier had now
taken place. The Lord's 'Holy One' had been placed in the grave,
but instead of his body decomposing it had been raised from
death.

According to the New Testament, it was St Peter on the day of
Pentecost who first applied this particular scripture to the resurrection of Jesus (Acts 2:27). It was to become a favourite one of the
early Church in their dialogue with the Jews, for it speaks of a
faithful servant of the Lord ('your Holy One') as having been
delivered from death. The word 'hell' in the Authorized Version
refers simply to 'death'. The word in Hebrew is *sheol*, which means
'grave' or 'the place of the departed'. There is no notion here of a
place of punishment or torment, such as most people associate
with the word 'hell'. The claim of the psalmist is that the Lord's
'Holy One' would not be left to rot in the grave, but that he would
enjoy 'the path of life' (v. 11).

However, as Peter tellingly pointed out to the Jewish pilgrims
gathered in Jerusalem that Pentecost, 'I may say to you confidently of our ancestor David that he both died and was buried, and
his tomb is with us to this day' (Acts 2:29). So the words couldn't
possibly apply to him. But, Peter went on, 'he [David] was a
prophet, he knew that God had sworn with an oath to him that he
would put one of his descendants on his throne. Foreseeing this,

David spoke of the resurrection of the Messiah, saying, "He was not abandoned to Hades, nor did his flesh experience corruption."' The words, he assured them, referred not to David, who was dead, but to Jesus, whom God had raised to life, a fact of which the apostles were themselves witnesses (see Acts 2:29–33).

So the words of the psalmist had been fulfilled. When God's true 'Holy One' appeared, the grave was powerless to claim him. Jesus died: there's no reasonable doubt about that. But 'it was impossible for death to keep its hold on him', as Peter explained to the crowd. The Son of God could not remain in the grave, because he is the Lord of life.

That was Peter's case for the resurrection, backed up, of course, by reliable eye-witnesses, himself included, who had met the risen Jesus. Far from being irrational and incredible, he claimed, if you thought about it in the light of God's promises, it was entirely predictable. There was, for him, an irresistible logic about the resurrection of Jesus.

For us, living in a period remote from the era of the prophets, and without the Jewish understanding that what has been prophesied has as good as happened already, things are not quite so straightforward. In a scientific era, we ask different questions about the resurrection. Was the tomb empty? If so, what had happened to the body of Jesus? Who or what was it that the apostles encountered: a ghost or spirit, perhaps, or an illusion, a self-deception? How could the body of the risen Jesus pass through locked doors if it was 'flesh and bones' as the Gospel claims?

For us, then, the crucial part of Peter's argument is not that the resurrection was prophesied and the prophecy was now fulfilled, but the sentence that followed: 'God has raised this Jesus to life, and we are all witnesses of the fact' (Acts 2:32). Our belief flows from the apostolic witness rather than the scriptural prophecy. We believe them when they say that they met Jesus truly and fully alive, 'body, mind and spirit', as we say, and we are prepared to put the other questions on hold until such time as we can understand in our own experience the meaning of 'resurrection life'.

Meanwhile, we have these words, forming a kind of link between the death on Friday and the new life of Sunday morning. 'But thou didst not leave his soul in hell [in the grave]; nor didst thou suffer thy Holy One to see corruption'. Every bit as much as the cross, the empty tomb and the risen Jesus are part of God's great purpose of salvation. It is that purpose which bridges the yawning gulf between death and life, between the darkness of Good Friday and the joy of Easter.

If it seemed to the onlookers on Good Friday that Jesus had been abandoned by his Father, the resurrection proves that nothing could be further from the truth. Even the disciples had to learn that it was through suffering and death that the promised redemption was to come, not despite them. Their scriptures might have given them the clue, but they read them with their minds closed. When the risen Jesus appeared to them, his first message was, in effect, 'I told you so. Why didn't you believe it?'

26

The risen, glorious king

Lift up your heads, O ye gates; and be ye lift up, ye
everlasting doors; and the King of glory shall come in. Who is
this King of glory? The Lord strong and mighty, the Lord
mighty in battle. Lift up your heads, O ye gates; and be ye lift
up, ye everlasting doors; and the King of glory shall come in.
Who is this King of glory? The Lord of hosts, he is the King
of glory.

Psalm 24:7–10

The greater the opposition, the greater the victory. And the greater the victory, the greater the honour.

The contrast with the picture of the lonely, suffering Jesus on the cross could not be greater. Having raided the Hebrew scriptures for the language of despair, abandonment and desolation, *Messiah* now turns to the Psalms for the language of victory and glory. The one who suffered and died is now revealed as the mighty victor. Death and darkness had done their worst, yet the Son of God triumphed over them.

This is the language of coronation. The Psalm may well have been sung when the ark of God was first brought into Jerusalem by King David, or it may have been composed for the coronation of a subsequent king. Either way, it describes a procession making its way to the gates of the city, the enthusiastic supporters of the king cheering and singing their way up the slopes leading to the walls, and being challenged—presumably in a friendly, affirmative way—by the guardians of the city gates.

The supporters are chanting, 'Get those gates open wide, as wide as you can make them! The King of Glory wants to enter the city!'

The guardians respond, as sentries traditionally always have: 'Who is this "King of Glory"? Name him, please, so that we can decide whether he can enter.'

The crowds outside respond enthusiastically. 'He's the Lord strong and mighty, the Lord mighty in battle.' And they follow that by repeating their earlier demand: 'Come on, get the gates open—in fact, you may have to enlarge them, because he is so great that your pathetic little gates may well be too small!'

The sentries repeat their question. 'Who is he, this "King of Glory"?' to be met by an even more precise reply: 'The Lord of hosts—the Captain of the armies!' Presumably at that point the gates were opened, and the procession wound its way into the narrow streets of the city and on to the temple.

There's little doubt that this Psalm is messianic. The 'king' in question may well have been David, or another actual monarch of history, but it obviously also looks on to the great day when the Lord's own anointed one would enter Jerusalem in triumph. The description of the king as 'the Lord strong and mighty' is not as odd as it might seem, for the concept of God as 'King' and the kings of his people as his vice-regents was strong in the Israel of the time. The king in some way 'represented' the Lord, ruling over the people only by God's appointment and anointing. His authority was God's, and his strength and glory were God's too.

And what was true of their earthly monarchs was doubly true of the Messiah. He would be the truly anointed one, who would reveal the glory and power and justice of God as never before. No wonder the gates needed to be stretched open to their limits!

'The Lord of hosts'—the 'Lord God of Sabaoth' of the 'Te Deum'—is the divine ruler or general of the armies (the 'hosts'). By extension, that came to mean not only the One who led the armies of Israel and fought for them, but the One who commanded the heavenly hosts, the 'winged squadrons of the skies', the angel-army.

And now, *Messiah* suggests, Jesus who died is being crowned with these particular honours. The man who was reviled and abused on the cross is shown to be the Lord of glory. The one who declined to call the angel-army to his aid (Matthew 26:53) is revealed as the Lord of the heavenly hosts. The one who seemed to be defeated by human evil and the power of death is none other than the victor over sin and the grave. No wonder the music soars!

A REFLECTION

The King of Glory—the 'Lord of hosts'—never batters his way into the city of the human heart. If the gates are closed, he waits until they are opened. It is only by invitation that he assumes the Lordship of our lives.

27

The Son of God

Unto which of the angels said he at any time, Thou art my Son, this day have I begotten thee? Let all the angels of God worship him.

Hebrews 1:5-6

Thou art gone up on high, thou hast led captivity captive, and received gifts for men: yea, even for thine enemies, that the Lord God might dwell among them.

Psalm 68:18 (BCP)

In a great household, the son and heir has more honour than even the most distinguished courtiers; in heaven the Son of God receives the worship of the entire heavenly 'household'.

There's no disguising the fact that this recitative, chorus and solo present formidable problems in terms of biblical interpretation. Partly this is caused by Jennens' habit of joining together what God has kept asunder! For instance, the first words of God ('Thou art my Son, this day have I begotten thee') are separated in the book of Hebrews from the quite different idea that on the occasion of the birth of Jesus the 'angels of God worshipped him'. The first quotation is from Psalm 2:7, and while it is a great favourite with New Testament writers, cited in Mark, Luke, Matthew, Acts and Romans, it is never applied to the birth of Jesus at Bethlehem, for the obvious reason that the early Christians firmly believed in the pre-existence of the Son of God. For them, as for Christians subsequently, this messianic prophecy speaks of the 'begetting' of the Son before the creation of the world— indeed, as affirming his eternal existence. As the Creed says, 'Eternally begotten of the Father, God from God, Light from Light, true God from true God, begotten not made, of one Being with the Father'.

But the second saying, 'Let all the angels of God worship him' was regularly applied by the early Church to the worship offered by the 'heavenly host' at the birth of Jesus in Bethlehem (Luke 2:13). In Hebrews it is preceded by the words, 'when he [God] brings the first-born into the world, he says...', making the connection with the nativity of Jesus specific. This saying is a particularly fascinating one for biblical scholars, incidentally, because it doesn't occur at all in the Hebrew Bible, but only in the 'Septuagint' (Greek) version of the scriptures, where it is found in Deuteronomy 32:43. Its authenticity was only finally established by the discovery of the Dead Sea Scrolls text fifty years ago (see, for example, footnote in NIV).

I'm sorry to introduce such complicated problems of interpretation! But the good news is that, once we have separated these two sayings in our minds, the idea behind them can come across with clarity. The Son is greater than the angels. The angels are 'ministers' (Hebrews 1:7) or 'servants', but Jesus is the Son. On earth he took upon himself the role of a servant, it's true, but by his nature he retained the glory and dignity of the Son of God. After the resurrection, this glory and dignity were recognized. As St Paul puts it in the opening verses of his Letter to the Romans, '[Jesus] was descended from David according to the flesh and was declared to be Son of God with power according to the spirit of holiness by resurrection from the dead.'

Messiah tells us nothing of the empty tomb or the men and women who were witnesses to the resurrection of Jesus. There is no road to Emmaus, no lake-side encounter, no surprise and joy in the Upper Room. Instead, we are transported to the heavenly realms, and invited to see what we might call the cosmic consequences of the resurrection. The earthly details are taken for granted, while we stand with the angels and join in their celebration of the fulfilment of God's purpose in sending Jesus to earth.

Part of that purpose is captured vividly in the other scripture cited here, from Psalm 68. This is a hymn of triumph—possibly a celebration of a notable victory over the enemy. It visualizes the King-Messiah as ascending the holy mountain (probably Jerusalem), leading the miserable captives he has won through his victory. There are 'gifts', too, presumably either tribute taken from the conquered, or gifts of thanksgiving offered to God in the temple. And the implication is that these 'gifts' will even bring blessing to the 'enemies'.

Let it be admitted that the meaning of the words 'even for thine enemies' is formidably obscure, so obscure, indeed, that one great Old Testament scholar, Albright, said, 'I have no idea what to do with them'! But the early Church had its own ideas, and their interpretation probably influenced Jennens. St Paul cited these verses in his letter to the Ephesians, arguing that when Christ 'ascended on high' he 'gave gifts to men', and that those gifts were the various gifts of ministry—apostles, prophets, evangelists, pastors, teachers. The gifts came about because Christ 'led captives in his train'—that is, 'led captivity captive'. Having conquered the power of evil, Christ could now distribute to his people the gifts that would enable them to carry that victory into the unbelieving world. In that way, 'the Lord God might dwell among them'—the knowledge of the love and power of God would be shared even with erstwhile 'enemies'.

These verses constitute a song of victory, a victory won through suffering and death, but a victory none the less. The eventual outcome of the war between good and evil has been decided, even if the 'mopping-up' operation is long and arduous. No one can change the result.

A clergyman friend of mine had to take a wedding on the Saturday afternoon when the team he had supported all his life was playing in the Cup Final. He left his ten-year old son, also a fervent supporter, watching it, and dashed back to the vicarage as quickly as he decently could. To his relief the match was still on, and he could see from the top of the screen that his side was winning one-nil. There couldn't be long to go—so why wasn't his son more excited? 'Look, look,' my friend shouted, 'We're going to win! Why aren't you on your feet shouting for them?'

'Relax, dad,' the boy replied. 'We have won. This is a replay.'

A REFLECTION

Battles, warrior-kings, angel hosts and captives in chains may seem very remote from the world we inhabit. Our images of conflict are more likely to be about strikes, board room battles, crime and police. But we know what it is to face dark and powerful enemies, and none are darker or more powerful than sin and death. And we understand what victory means, and its consequences. Messiah is celebrating the greatest victory in the history of creation, the conquest of those two deadly enemies. While that victory is assured—no one can 'change the result'—it still has to be experienced by the people for whom it took place. The gifts of the ascended King are to help us in that task.

The company of preachers

The Lord gave the word: great was the company of the preachers.

Psalm 68:11 (BCP)

How beautiful are the feet of them that preach the gospel of peace, and bring glad tidings of good things! Their sound is gone out into all lands, and their words to the ends of the world.

Romans 10:15, 18

If the message is really good, it doesn't matter what the messenger is like!

I suspect that Jennens had part of St Paul's letter to the church at Ephesus in mind when he pulled together these fascinating ideas from Psalm 68 and another of the apostle's letters, the one to Rome. In Ephesians (4:8) Paul quotes from this very Psalm: 'When he ascended on high he made captivity a captive; he gave gifts to his people' (v. 18). That is the idea which we have come across already—the King-Messiah conquering his enemies and taking tribute from them, which he then distributes to his jubilant followers. But Paul gives it a specific application. The 'gifts', he says, are those of the ascended Christ to the Church—the gift of apostleship, the gift of prophecy, the gift of an evangelist, pastor or teacher. So he links the ascension of the risen Christ with the gifts necessary for continuing his work on earth.

And a central part of that work, indeed *the* central part, is to bring the good news of Christ's victory to the whole world. After all, that was the last command of the risen Jesus. 'Go into all the world and proclaim the good news to the whole creation' (Mark); 'Go... and make disciples of all nations' (Matthew); 'You will be my witnesses' (Acts).

'The Lord gave the word.' It is, as St Mark calls it, 'good news of God' (Mark 1:14). It is the unfolding of his purpose for the whole of mankind, now revealed through the Messiah. Jesus completed the work that his Father had given him to do (John 17:4) but the task remains of announcing the good news. It took only one man, though admittedly that one was the Son of God, to gain our salvation, but it will require a 'great company' to take the news of it to the whole world.

So it is a daunting task. It even seems daunting today, with access to mass communication and worldwide transport. It must have looked virtually impossible in the world of the first century AD. Yet, fired with the Holy Spirit, that original handful of men and women did what they were told. Sent out from Jerusalem, they trudged across burning deserts, risked their lives in boats at sea and faced persecution and torture. They stood before emperors and kings. They crossed continents and oceans with their message. And slowly at first, then with mounting success, they began to win the ancient world for Christ.

Their 'feet' were 'beautiful'. The imagery is Isaiah's, but Paul applies it to the Christian missionaries as they set out on their new commission. He presumably didn't mean that the feet of the disciples were any more beautifully formed than anyone else's! But the feet brought the message, and the message was beautiful beyond words. After all, they brought good news of peace to war-torn hearts and a war-torn world. Through his death Jesus Christ had made peace: peace with God, and then peace between people. As we have seen, the price was enormous—the shedding of his blood. But the result was beautiful, and those who bore the message were themselves transformed by it.

A REFLECTION

Christ's followers are still called to be messengers of the good news. But if people are to receive and believe it, they will need to see that it has already had its effect on the messengers. In fact, to some extent the messengers are the message, because the good news is largely judged by the lives of those who bring it.

THE MESSIAH KING

A t this point *Messiah* pauses, as it were, to celebrate the coronation of Jesus, and to look at its consequences. If the Son of God has truly conquered sin and death, and is now exalted to the 'right hand of the majesty on high', what does that mean to a world where evil and darkness have held sway for so long?

The Ascension is a neglected festival in many parts of the Christian Church today. Easter speaks of victory over death and the grave. We can understand and appreciate that. Pentecost speaks of the power God makes available in the Church and in believers to enable us to live in step with his purposes. That sounds excellent! But the Ascension seems more elusive. Why does it matter that the risen Jesus was 'taken up'—in the picture language of the New Testament—to the 'right hand of God'? We know he was the Son of God. We know his resurrection represented a mighty victory over darkness. How would this symbolic 'coronation' add anything to it?

The answer lies in the airs, recitative and choruses that follow, with words taken from the Psalms and the book of Revelation. The seating of Christ at his Father's right hand is a sign of completed victory, and of the Father's approval of it. Christ has 'sat down' because his arduous work is done, but he sits 'at the right hand' because that is the place of highest honour. But as yet not all people will accept that the battle is over, and not all people will recognize its inevitable consequences.

29

Rebel hearts and minds

*Why do the nations so furiously rage together: why do the
people imagine a vain thing? The kings of the earth rise up,
and the rulers take counsel together: against the Lord, and
against his Anointed.*

Psalm 2:1–2 (BCP)

**While God seemed powerless, the powers that be were content to lie
low. But when God showed his hand and threatened their authority
the powers of earth revealed themselves in all their ugliness.**

The cross and resurrection of Jesus are, in the end, about power.
Who rules the universe? Who holds sway on earth? Where does
ultimate power lie? While Jesus was dying on the cross, his disciples could have been forgiven for feeling that, yet again, the evil
forces of the world were shown to be more powerful than goodness, truth and love. Here was a man who preached forgiveness,
turning the other cheek, loving one's enemies. More than that, he
showed extraordinary power himself in casting out evil, in healing
the sick, in bringing sight to the blind. If ever anyone could challenge the might of worldly power and empire, surely it would be
him?

And yet it seemed to have ended in failure. It was the Roman
Governor, the representative of imperial power, who pronounced
the death penalty. His soldiers carried it out, urged on by the religious authorities of Jerusalem. This was the hour of darkness, the
moment when all hope had gone. If Jesus couldn't overcome the
'principalities and powers', then surely nobody could?

That is why the resurrection of Jesus is such a dramatic rever-
sal—so dramatic that it took the bewildered disciples by surprise.
In one moment of divine intervention, history was re-written.
What had seemed defeat was revealed as victory. And those who
had seemed invincible in their might and authority were shown to
be mere mortals after all.

This Psalm captures the flavour of it exactly. It pictures the
Lord's Anointed, the Messiah-King (for that is precisely what the
title means) as the object of earthly rage and fury. The powers that
be conspire and involve people in complicated plots, all with the

object of confounding the purpose of God. But their plots are in vain. Their rule is about to be taken from them and given to another, the 'Lord's Anointed'. When the words were first penned it was a picture of the victory of a king of Israel against the scheming and plotting of the Gentile nations surrounding them. But now it becomes, in the mystery of prophecy, a picture of the victory of Jesus over the assembled powers of earth and of death and the grave. However much the enemies of God rage or scheme and plot, and however great their power appears to be, God has defeated them.

What is true on this vast, macro scale, in terms of the victory of God over the evil in his universe, is also true on the micro scale of personal experience. It is a real breakthrough in faith when we see all the powers and influences that line up against the Christian believer through the perspectives of eternity. All the cynicism and ridicule, all the temptations of money, sex and power, all the manipulation and persecutions we may experience at the hands of those whose eyes are closed to what God has done, are really only minor skirmishes in the context of the whole battle. Christ has conquered. He has gone up on high. He is seated on the throne of the universe.

That doesn't mean that the fury of the enemy may not hurt us. It doesn't mean that we don't need to be aware of the conspiracies and plots of those who have most to lose by God's victory over evil. But it does mean that we can see them as they really are, 'kings' and 'people' whose day is very nearly over and whose defeat has already taken place.

A REFLECTION

In Western society we may feel that much of the opposition to God's rule flows from apathy and scepticism rather than direct, angry opposition. Yet whenever people seek to witness to Christian values or challenge the world's priorities the reaction—however it expresses itself—is just as negative and often vicious. God and 'Mammon' are still on collision course, and God's people need to be clear which side of the conflict they are on!

30

Breaking against the rock

Let us break their bonds asunder: and cast away their yokes from us. He that dwelleth in heaven shall laugh them to scorn: the Lord shall have them in derision.

Psalm 2:3–4 (BCP)

When it comes to 'bonds' and 'yokes', the important question is, Who placed them on us, and why? It might be better to be the subject of a good King than a free man under a bad one.

One of the first rules for interpreting a passage of scripture is to ask, 'Who said it?' In this case the answer is absolutely crucial. It was the 'heathen' and the 'kings of the earth' and the 'rulers' who had been plotting against the Lord and his Anointed One who now called on each other to join in one last effort to throw off his rule—that is, God's rule. The bonds and the yokes are the means by which the Lord had restrained their evil intentions and brought them under his control. The call here, in other words, is to rebellion against God.

The psalmist regards the very idea as ridiculous. The 'one who sitteth in heaven' simply laughs at their threats and plots, like Gulliver laughing at the tiny Lilliputians who tried to tie him down. These petty tyrants may have their day, strutting around their castle walls and reviewing their troops, but the throne of the universe is not up for grabs. If they set themselves against God, there can only be one result in the end.

This is not, of course, the kind of language with which present-day Christians are comfortable. To us it sounds almost dangerously triumphalist. We live in a world that has to a considerable extent ceased to believe that anybody 'rules the universe', and would regard our claim that God is in charge as little more than whistling in the dark. For most people, it doesn't look as though anyone is in control of things, least of all a good and loving God. But there is considerable apprehension about various powerful forces in the wings—science and technology, for instance, and giant commercial interests. For us, these are the 'powers', the 'rulers' and the 'kings of the earth'; it is in their hands that real power lies, not in some invisible, unknown and unrecognized

God. Like the people of Israel, we may well fear what they are doing, or might do—the Frankenstein's monsters created in secret laboratories, the schemes to exploit the world's riches for the advantage of the few and the impoverishment of the many, the insidious elimination of personal responsibility and individual value.

Faced with these real and tangible fears, perhaps we ought to listen to the psalmist. Though people seek to break the bonds of natural and moral law which God has built into our society, the consequences for those who do it are too awful to contemplate. Though the world in its cleverness sees no need of God, that doesn't mean that he has suddenly ceased to exist!

The world has a Maker, and there are Maker's Instructions to go with it. Like anyone with a new piece of apparatus in their hands, we can if we wish ignore the Maker's Instructions and behave as if they don't exist. But many of us have found to our cost that if we do, the result is disastrous. If you own a dish-washer there's no law to stop you putting WD40 in the rinse-aid container. After all, it's yours—you paid for it. But if you do, and the thing simply won't work properly, you can't then blame the maker. God who made the world has also given us our 'instructions'—his natural and moral laws, and the voice of conscience. If we ignore them, then the consequences are... well, what we are seeing so widely today. It is no use blaming God for what is a matter of human responsibility.

The psalmist's language may indeed be triumphalist, but there's no harm in reminding ourselves that there is still the 'One in the heavens', and all these human pretensions are simply empty posturing to him. To 'break his bonds' and 'cast away his yoke' may seem like freedom, but in fact it is the road to disaster.

As *Messiah* makes clear, simply by placing them at this point in the story, the resurrection and ascension of Jesus have given new weight to these words. What the people of Israel believed by faith, or on the evidence of past blessing, the people of the new covenant can believe because the uniquely Anointed One, Jesus, has defeated our greatest enemies, death and sin, and been placed on the glorified right hand of his Father. As this Psalm puts it, 'I have set my king on Zion, my holy hill' (Psalm 2:6). It is a song of coronation.

*Individual freedom is a very precious thing, but like all valuable
things it can be misused. As the old prayer says, 'His service is
perfect freedom'. There is a surrender of sovereignty which does not
involve the loss of freedom, and that is surrender to God. After all,
as we have seen, 'his yoke is easy'.*

31

The iron sceptre of love

Thou shalt break them with a rod of iron; thou shalt dash them in pieces like a potter's vessel.

Psalm 2:9

Those who set themselves to oppose God are destined for destruction, not because that gives him pleasure but because it is inevitable. There is only room for one Ruler of the created order.

Messiah takes one last look at the awful consequences facing those who set themselves up against the God who raised Jesus from the dead and enthroned him in heaven. The words are still from Psalm 2, and in their context speak of God's judgment of the heathen powers who have opposed Israel. Their armies are terrible, their chariots awesome: but the God of Israel will break them with his iron rod—a mace, possibly, or a kingly sceptre—and dash them in pieces like a piece of unwanted pottery.

The Septuagint (Greek) version of this Psalm has the word 'shepherd' instead of 'break'—only a slight alteration of the Hebrew word would be needed to give the alternative reading. It would then read, 'Thou shalt shepherd them with a rod of iron'—in other words, even the heathen nations will eventually come under the Lord's rule and protection. But in both cases what is involved is submission to his kingly rule, represented by the rod or sceptre.

The secondary image, of the smashed pot, carries the same message. When the potter has shaped the clay and it is still moist he can re-make it. But once it is fired, it cannot be re-shaped. If a flaw is found in it at that stage, there is nothing to do with it but to smash it and start again. People in the ancient world would have been familiar with the potter at his wheel, and with the pile of smashed rejects lying beside him.

Indeed, the potter is a familiar image in the Bible. Isaiah, Jeremiah and Ezekiel, the great prophets of Israel, all use the potter and his work as pictures of God's work with us. St Paul picks up the same idea in Romans, 1 Corinthians and 2 Timothy. God creates us, like the potter shaping the clay—the idea goes right back to the creation story in Genesis (2:7). While the process of shaping our lives is in progress, we can be re-made at his hands. But a time comes when the clay sets hard, and if the vessel is then found to be defective it is beyond redemption—it is 'dashed in pieces'.

In this Psalm that idea is spelt out in verse 12: 'Kiss the Son, lest he be angry, and ye perish from the way, when his wrath is kindled but a little'. The strange phrase 'kiss the Son' might mean 'kiss his feet'—that is, in submission to his rule. In other words, make your peace while you can, before the moment comes when it is too late. The same idea is often conveyed in the Bible by the image of 'hardening'. Again, the potter's work is used as a warning. To 'harden our hearts' against God's love and mercy is to risk the possibility that repentance, if it comes at all, will be too late. The marred vessel will have to be rejected, 'dashed in pieces'.

Of course, this is not an aspect of God's dealings with people which we like to dwell on. Indeed, we know from the teaching of Jesus that God's intention is our redemption, not our judgment. 'The Lord… is patient with you, not wanting any to perish, but all to come to repentance' (2 Peter 3:9). Yet even there the warning is clear: do not presume on the patience of God. 'The day of the Lord will come like a thief.'

If we are tempted to think that the idea of God himself actually 'hardening' anyone's heart contradicts his stated purpose of bringing everyone to redemption, it might help to reflect on a curious natural phenomenon. If you put a lump of butter and a lump of clay out under a hot sun, you will see that one melts and the other hardens. But it is the same sun in both cases. The difference lies in the material it works on. Cold, unbelieving hearts are hardened, even by God's love. Warm, trusting hearts are melted by it.

The Messiah has come to save those who put their trust in him. He has done everything that is necessary to make that possible. The offer of grace is made to all, and the messengers have been sent out on beautiful feet to carry the invitation to the ends of the earth. The gates of his kingdom are open, but he will not compel us to come in. Hard hearts need to be melted by his love, rebellious wills need to submit to his kingly rule. We are to 'kiss the feet' of the Son of God and make our peace with him… and not to put it off any longer.

Kingly sceptres and rods of iron are not familiar concepts for Christians today, but Jesus spoke more about the 'kingdom of God'—the rule of God in the lives of men and women—than he did about anything else. Submitting to the rule of one who loves us, and above anything else desires our good, is not demeaning but rewarding.

32

King of kings

Hallelujah: for the Lord God omnipotent reigneth. The
kingdom of this world is become the kingdom of our Lord and
of his Christ; and he shall reign for ever and ever. KING OF
KINGS, AND LORD OF LORDS.

Revelation 19:6; 11:15; 19:16

The final proof of the victory of God will be his actual reign over
what had been rebel territory—the 'kingdom of the world'.

In his space fiction book *Out of the Silent Planet*, C.S. Lewis gives
his hero, Ransom, a view of earth from a distant planet. It is only
slowly that he comes to understand that Earth, which he knew
and loved so well, is in fact a rebel planet, the only one in all creation that has defied its Creator. For all its beauty, and all the love
and happiness that humans often experience, this is not a perfect
world.

It was created perfectly, of course. But human beings used the
free will which God gave them to reject his will. The subsequent
history of the human race is the story of the struggle between our
divine origins—'made in the image of God'—and the damaging
effects of wilful disobedience.

The story of the Bible is the slow unfolding of God's purpose
for his rebel planet. The purpose reached its climax in the coming of the promised Saviour, the Messiah. Jesus clearly saw his
mission as one of directly combating the forces of evil which held
God's creatures in their power. But of course he did more than
demonstrate his power over evil in the lives of individuals. He saw
the cross as the moment when the 'powers of darkness' would
have their final moment of triumph—a temporary triumph,
because the resurrection of Jesus would change the picture deci-
sively. What had looked like defeat was victory: God's victory over
the power that had gripped what the Bible calls 'the children of
disobedience'.

We have seen how *Messiah* has marked the implications of that
victory. The enemies of God have been put to shame. The people
of God have been vindicated in their faith. The promises of God,
which had seemed so far-fetched, have been marvellously ful-

filled. And the Son of God, the 'Anointed One', has been honoured by his Father, being placed in the seat of the triumphant conqueror at his monarch's right hand. We have had the themes of that victory spelt out. Now we are called to join in the Coronation Anthem.

The 'Hallelujah Chorus' is obviously the best-known piece in the whole work. In 1996 it was voted into tenth place by over 70,000 listeners to Britain's leading classical music station when they were invited to name their favourite piece of music. We are all familiar with it as a vast song of triumph, hammered out by a thousand voices with swelling organ or full orchestra. What is less well appreciated is its message, because it is much, much more than merely a noisy piece of religious jingoism.

Its first word is Hebrew: 'hallelujah!' It means, simply, 'praise the Lord'. It is a call to worship, certainly, but it is also an expression of personal gratitude. That's the way many Christians use it today. Instead of saying 'thank goodness' or even 'thank God' they say 'praise the Lord'. In other words, if something has gone well, a prayer has been answered, a crisis or challenge overcome or a danger passed, 'give the praise and thanks to God, not me'.

It has been very heart-warming at great athletic games in recent years to see the many fine Christian competitors bursting through the tape ahead of their rivals and then either falling to their knees or throwing their hands in the air to give thanks to God. It's as though they are saying, 'Yes, I won the race, but it was the Lord who gave me the power and strength to do it. So give him the praise, not me!'

When Mother Teresa received an international prize for 'services to religion' she accepted the cheque, but then turned and laid it on the altar behind her and, as the audience began to clap, knelt in front of it with her hands upraised. 'Praise the Lord—hallelujah!' says quite simply 'Give God the glory'. The Hallelujah Chorus is a fitting climax to the oratorio's reflection on the results of Christ's victory because it sets it so firmly in the purpose of God. What he planned has come to pass. The rescue operation for his rebellious creatures has been totally successful, and his divine emissary has returned to his side with the spoils of victory.

The rest of the chorus celebrates some of those 'spoils'. 'The Lord God omnipotent reigneth.' God always reigned over his creation, of course. He has never been less than 'omnipotent'—all-powerful—even though in mercy and patience he held back from destroying his rebel children. But now his power has been fully revealed. Even death and the grave, which seem so formidable to mortal beings, have been forced to yield to him. And the evil which had seemed to have the world in its grip has been judged and defeated.

The Lord can't be raised higher than he is already, whatever some hymns may say! God can't be greater than God has always been. But of course he can be given a greater place in our lives and in our worship. As Herbert's hymn says, 'In my heart, though not in heaven, I can raise him'. A recognition that 'he has the whole world in his hands'—which is easier to sing than to believe—can be a life-changing experience.

The other great thought here is that the 'kingdom of this world'—society organized as though God did not exist, literally, the 'secular kingdom'—has become 'the kingdom of our Lord and of his Christ'. While the whole universe is God's by creation, this world and its people have resisted his rule. That doesn't mean that God has abandoned us, or that his grace and love are not still active in the world, but that human society as an entity is not God-centred. The briefest glance at life around us should convince us of the truth of that.

But now, through the victory of Jesus, that kingdom, too, is brought back into God's 'commonwealth'. That doesn't mean that all the signs and symptoms of rebellion have been eradicated, but that the final destiny of the human race has changed direction. From the time of Christ's ascension there is a fundamental difference in the relationship of the world to God. We are now a redeemed world and a redeemed people. 'The kingdom of this world has become the kingdom of our Lord and of his Christ.' He is 'King of kings and Lord of lords'—all earthly powers and rulers come under his sovereignty.

'And he shall reign for ever and ever.' This is no temporary revolution. Things have changed, in every sense of the phrase, for good. That is why Christians should be optimists! We sing, 'God is working his purpose out, as year succeeds to year', but the real difference is when we start to live as though it is true. We are not the minority survivors of a desperate rescue attempt, as some seem to have believed, but the first-fruits of a marvellous and vast harvest of salvation.

The victory of Jesus on the cross has both cosmic and personal consequences. It is very wonderful that because of what he did I can be forgiven and accepted by God. It is even more wonderful that through the same event the whole history of the world has been transformed. Both in my life and in the life of the human race of which I am a tiny part, 'the Lord reigns'.

LIFE THROUGH THE MESSIAH

Having celebrated the victory of the Messiah in a cosmic sense, we now turn to the consequences of that victory in our own lives. In some ways this is the theology of the whole oratorio applied to the life of the individual Christian. And for once the message is drawn not from the Hebrew prophets or Psalms, but from the writings of the apostle Paul—though with an important 'overture' from the book of Job.

For St Paul the resurrection of Jesus made a difference to everything. It proved that Jesus was the Son of God (Romans 1:4). It represented God's victory over the forces of evil in the universe (Colossians 2:15). But it also guaranteed to those who are 'in Christ' a part in his resurrection. Because God raised Jesus from the dead, we too can be raised from death. In 'Adam', in our humanity, we are destined to die; 'in Christ' we shall be made alive (1 Corinthians 15:22).

It's hard to think of anywhere in sacred song that this fundamental Christian truth is expressed as powerfully as it is here. The rather complex arguments of the apostle seem to be clarified by the sheer lucidity of the music! And all through this section runs a note of deep faith and confidence.

Modern Christianity has at times found it hard to hold on to belief in life after death. The very notion has been ridiculed by unbelievers as 'pie in the sky when you die', whereas contemporary man wants 'cake on the plate while you wait'. Christians have not wanted to sound over-confident in an area where none of us has personal experience to support faith. In the nature of things, there is rather a shortage of people who have come back from the dead to tell us about it.

But one has, and his name is Jesus. It is because of him, and because of his resurrection from the dead, that we can hold confidently to the truths which St Paul regarded as foundational.

After all, as he says, 'If Christ has not been raised, your faith is futile... But in fact Christ has been raised from the dead, the first fruits of those who have died' (1 Corinthians 15:17, 20). Jesus, in other words, is the beginning of a vast harvest of all those who will rise from death. That is the 'mystery' to which the words of *Messiah* now turn their attention.

33

And after this?

I know that my redeemer liveth, and that he shall stand at the latter day upon the earth: And though worms destroy this body, yet in my flesh shall I see God.

Job 19:25–26

In the face of the 'last enemy', we need alongside us the One who has defeated him.

There is something about the way Handel has pitched the word 'know' that is marvellously reassuring. It makes the whole statement revolve around the conviction of the speaker: 'I know'. In its context in the oratorio, it echoes the Christian conviction that because Christ lives, we shall live. That is the proper way round. Belief in life beyond death flows from the resurrection of Jesus, not the other way round. No arguments or evidences carry much weight apart from the empty tomb and risen life of the Saviour.

That is the context of these words in *Messiah*. In the book of Job, from which they are taken, the context is very different. Job is replying to his unhelpful 'comforters'. He recognizes that his plight is wretched, that his friends have deserted him, that physically he is 'nothing but skin and bones'. Yet, in this brave statement of faith, he asserts that he believes that he has a 'redeemer' or 'defender'—someone who will stand by him and deliver him from his plight. Eventually this person will emerge, and in the end—perhaps only on the other side of the grave—he will 'see God', and God's justice, which he feels has abandoned him at the moment.

I think that's what it probably means, but to be honest the passage is incredibly obscure and can be translated in about ten different ways! It seems very unlikely that Job was claiming that his flesh and blood would be restored after being 'destroyed' by death, and that 'in his flesh' he would appear before God in heaven. If he was saying that, then it is a belief about death and resurrection virtually unknown to the rest of the Hebrew Scriptures.

Yet clearly this was (however it's to be translated) a ringing declaration of faith in God's ultimate justice, even though it would only be revealed after death. It's also a statement of faith in a 'redeemer', a figure like the 'kinsman-redeemer' of Jewish culture—the relative who would come to your help in a time of desperate need. Both are powerful ideas. Both found their fulfilment in Jesus Christ, the Messiah.

Consequently, whatever the original language may or may not have meant, these words express Christian hope and faith with great eloquence. We do know that our redeemer is alive. That is a central truth of our faith. We do believe that in the end he will stand on earth again. We do believe in the 'resurrection of the body', though not, it has to be said, in the reassembly of our present one after corruption, worms or fire have done their work! We believe in resurrection, not resuscitation. As St Paul says, 'Flesh and blood cannot inherit the kingdom of God' (1 Corinthians 15:50), but human beings in new, resurrection bodies will.

This idea is worked out in the words of the apostle over the next few recitatives, airs and choruses. They deal with profound issues which may seem unnecessarily complicated and abstruse to us. For myself, I have always found his line of argument persuasive and convincing, but I could quite understand someone who said that they preferred to stand on Job's unequivocal statement of faith which precedes it: 'I know that my redeemer liveth.' In one sense, St Paul and Job have the same message. Because my Redeemer lives, I believe that I shall live, and that one day I shall 'see God'.

A REFLECTION

Faith in life beyond death is not a matter of arguing a position but putting our trust in God and his 'Redeemer'.

34

Because he lives

For now is Christ risen from the dead, the firstfruits of them that sleep.

1 Corinthians 15:20

Since Jesus Christ rose from the dead, life beyond the grave is not a vague possibility. It has actually happened.

One of my most valued memories is of Easter Day in Ducklington, the Cotswold village where I was once the parish priest. It's an old Norman church set, like so many country churches, in the middle of a stone-walled graveyard. As the choir and ministers processed into a packed church, singing 'Jesus Christ is risen today', and the sunlight streamed through the wonderful Lady chapel window, the paradox struck me as it never had before. We were celebrating the victory of life over death in the middle of a graveyard!

Yet it didn't seem odd. Quite the contrary. It was as if all those past residents of the village, going back in some cases several hundred years, were joining us 'in glory' in our songs of Easter joy. They knew by experience what we believed by faith: Christ has risen, we are risen!

The Epistle that Easter morning was this passage from St Paul's letter to the church at Corinth. It has never spoken to me so powerfully. In the place of death we celebrated eternal life. Because Christ lives, 'them that sleep' will also live. He is the fore-runner of a measureless harvest of souls, to be joined one day by those of us who are at present alive on earth, the 'communion of saints', as the Creed calls it.

Messiah adds this verse to the end of the solo 'I know that my redeemer liveth', as though to stress the identity of that 'redeemer': he is the Christ who died and rose. Whatever Job's words meant, here is their fulfilment. Our Redeemer is alive. One day he will return. And because of what he has done for us, we shall see God.

The Christians at Corinth were clearly very anxious about their friends who had died. There was a general expectation in the early Church that Jesus would return very soon, certainly in their life-time. There were things that Jesus said which might have encouraged that view—see, for instance, Mark 9:1 and 13:30. But he hadn't returned, and they were worried that those Christians who had died might in some way 'miss out' on the blessings of the promised kingdom. This section of the letter—chapter 15—is really an extended answer to that fear.

First Paul sets out the evidence, coolly and clinically. 'I told you at the start what the gospel is', he says. 'Christ died for our sins, was buried, and was raised from death on the third day.' He was seen by Peter, by the Twelve, by James—and even by a crowd of five hundred people. So how could they doubt the reality of the resurrection of Jesus? Were they calling the apostles 'false witnesses'? 'If Christ has not been raised,' he argues, 'your faith is futile and you are still in your sins—and those Christians who have died are lost.'

'But Christ has indeed been raised from the dead, the firstfruits of those who have fallen asleep (in death).' That is the 'good news', and it is based on solid, verifiable evidence. Most of the witnesses of the resurrection, he assures them, are still alive. If you don't believe me, ask them!

So the faith of those Christians in Corinth nearly 2,000 years ago was based, as ours is, not just on hope, but on evidence. Job had the faith to visualize his 'redeemer' as a living reality, and to believe that one day he would himself 'see God'. The Christian has much, much more: the evidence of truthful witnesses, the existence, survival and growth of the Christian Church, the inward assurance of the Holy Spirit. Given all that, we should be able to speak with at least as much conviction as that man of God did so long ago: 'I know that my redeemer liveth'... and to believe it, even in the middle of a graveyard!

A REFLECTION

The resurrection of Jesus is not an optional extra tacked on to the end of the Christian story. Without it, the whole story is discredited. When God raised Jesus from death it was much more than a single, mighty act of deliverance to rescue his Son from the grip of death. It opened the flood-gates! From that time on, death's hold on the human race was broken. Jesus was the first, but by no means the last, of those who would pass through death into eternal life. That is the true message of comfort for those who mourn the loss of loved ones.

35

The second 'Adam'

Since by man came death, by man came also the resurrection of the dead. For as in Adam all die, even so in Christ shall all be made alive.

1 Corinthians 15:21–22

'O loving wisdom of our God! When all was sin and shame, a second Adam to the fight, and to the rescue came' (J.H. Newman).

The genius who invented inoculation had discovered one of life's great paradoxes: that the answer to the disease is often a bit of the disease itself. I suppose it's not dissimilar to the probably fallacious remedy for a hangover based on 'a hair of the dog that bit you'. More effectively, fire fights fire, we do know that. We use fire to clear a break in the woods to counter the blazing forest that is upwind.

The Bible often thinks of sin as a disease or infection, by now deeply rooted in human experience. That idea lies behind many of the Gospel stories of Jesus healing 'lepers'—not people infected with the modern disease of that name, but men and women who had contracted some highly contagious and disabling skin condition which seems to have been incurable by ordinary medicine. Sin is contagious. Sin embeds itself deeply into human lives. Indeed, in the language of the scriptures, sin kills: 'The wages of sin is death'.

So there is no suggestion in the language of the Bible that sin doesn't matter, or is simply a little failing or weakness to be lightly dismissed. Sin has wrecked our relationship with God, it has plagued our planet and torn apart our homes, communities and nations. Sin is not trivial but deeply serious, and like that 'leprosy' of old is contagious and eventually fatal.

And it all came about through 'a man'. St Paul, who wrote these words in the middle of a very profound argument about death and resurrection, was undoubtedly thinking of the story of the first man, 'Adam'. It was through human disobedience that sin entered the world. It was through 'a' man (rather than 'man') that death came. The first act of disobedience was simply the precursor of many more such acts. Humans—again, that is the word Paul uses, rather than 'males'—chose the path of disobedience, and it led to disaster.

However you choose to read the story of Adam and Eve in Genesis, it is a story of wilful rejection of God's commandments. The essential sin then, as now, was pride. Adam and Eve thought that they knew better than God. That is the real kernel of the story. And sin down the succeeding ages has had the same cause. We sin because we think we know better than God what is good for us. A little bit of envy doesn't matter. A smattering of deceit, a soupçon of anger, can't do any harm. Indeed, surely a touch of ambition and aggression are good things? And love (by which we mean lust) makes the world go round, doesn't it? It would be very narrow-minded of God to get upset over things we would regard as inconsequential.

But disobedience spells death. That is the message of the story of the Fall. Sin is a fatal infection in the life-blood of the human race. And it has come about not because of what God willed but because of what we have done. Death—spiritual death, separation from God—is the consequence of sin, and sin is a product of human decision. It is by 'a man' that death has come.

And it is by 'a man' that the victory over death has come, too. The music itself expresses the contrast. By the disobedience of a man sin entered the human condition, and that is a sad and sorry plight. But by the utter and complete obedience of another man— the Son of Man, Jesus—the consequences of that sin have been abolished, and that is a cause for joy in heaven.

St Paul contrasts two 'Adams'—the word simply means 'the man', or perhaps, representatively, 'The Man'. There was the Man who sinned, and brought death; and there is the Man who was sinless, and has brought life. What flowed from the first action was death; what flows from the second is life. That Christ, who was without sin, in some mysterious way died 'for sin' is the heart of the Gospel. 'For our sake [God] made him to be sin who knew no sin, so that in him we might become the righteousness of God' (2 Corinthians 5:21). Once again, the remedy for the disease was the disease itself, accepted, borne and defeated. That is the divine paradox of our redemption.

There is one possible confusion which can arise from these words, and that is about the little word 'all'. When it says that 'in Adam all die' it doesn't, and could not, mean that because one man at the dawn of history disobeyed God all the rest of us are now paying the consequences! Where would the principle of God's justice be in that scenario? Sin is not just something 'Adam' did, but something I do: it consists not just of being human, like him, but sinning, like him. 'As in Adam all die' means that everyone who is human shares Adam's mortal nature, because we share Adam's mortal weakness. There is a solidarity about sin!

When St Paul goes on to say that 'even so in Christ shall all be made alive' he is speaking of a second 'solidarity', the solidarity of salvation. Everyone who shares in Adam's moral failure shares his fate; everyone who shares in Christ's moral victory shares his risen life.

To be 'in Christ' is Pauline language for being a Christian, a baptized believer, a true member of the body of Christ. That is the new solidarity, and it is one which replaces the old 'Adamic' solidarity. We can be taken out of the fellowship of sin and death and brought into the fellowship of forgiveness and life. But whereas everybody, without exception, is 'in Adam', just by being born into the human race, it is only those who have been 'born again' of water and the Spirit who are 'in Christ'. The distinction is a very important one!

A REFLECTION

'God is not willing that any should perish.' The dreadful consequences of sin hang like a fatal cloud over the human race. But in sending Jesus, God has altered the situation fundamentally. It is not only that sin can be forgiven, but that sin has been defeated. As the hymn puts it, 'Be of sin the double cure, Cleanse me from its guilt and power'.

36

The secret revealed

Behold, I tell you a mystery; We shall not all sleep, but we shall all be changed, In a moment, in the twinkling of an eye, at the last trumpet.

1 Corinthians 15:51–52

Some Christians will be changed through death, and some Christians will be changed while still in mortal flesh. But we can be sure of one thing: if we are to enter the kingdom of God, we shall first have to undergo a radical transformation.

This short recitative serves as a link between the previous chorus, which speaks of the certainty of eternal life in Christ, to the following solo, which looks on to the dramatic events of the Day of Judgment. Here the apostle is dealing with two questions which are clearly uppermost in the minds of his readers. Firstly, will all this happen while we are still alive on earth? And secondly, as he has just said that 'flesh and blood cannot inherit the kingdom of heaven' (v. 50), what will happen to those still in their mortal bodies when all of this occurs?

In answer, St Paul offers to unfold a 'mystery'. The word has overtones for us of the 'mysterious'—something that can never be understood or explained. But the Greek word he used, *musterion*, has no such connotations. It doesn't mean a puzzle which we can't ever hope to solve, but a secret which human beings can never wholly grasp unless God reveals it to them. Now, says Paul, that 'mystery' can be unwrapped. I can let you into the secret, a secret hidden until then in the purposes of God.

What is that 'secret'? It is nothing less than the total transformation of every believer. Those who die are transformed by the process of death. Their bodies disappear like a seed in the ground (v. 37), but they are given new, resurrection bodies at the 'last day'. Christians who are still alive at the second coming of Christ will never experience death—that is the meaning of 'we shall not all sleep'. But they, too, will be transformed: not by death, but by an instant moment of re-creation. In the 'twinkling of an eye' (literally, 'at an eye's glance') they will be released from their mortal bodies and 'clothed' in new, resurrection ones. Then all of them—

those who were alive and those who had died—will be on a completely equal footing, fully equipped for life in the kingdom of heaven.

This will happen, he says, 'at the last trumpet'. Trumpet blasts generally denote victory and triumph in the story of Israel—think of the capture of Jericho, when it was the blast of the instruments that brought the walls 'tumbling down'. But the sound of the trumpet was also associated with the 'Day of the Lord'. It would be like a herald calling people to the throne of ultimate justice, to the great moment of decision. Both ideas are probably found here. The sound of the trumpet will signal the end of things as we have always known them. We shall never return to the sort of life we live now. But it will also usher in the moment of truth, when the great and small, the living and the dead, the people of every nation, language and culture will stand before their Maker.

At that moment, for St Paul, there is nothing to fear for those who are 'in Christ'. After all, these words are not meant to be a warning, but a comfort. Those we have loved who have gone before us in the sleep of death will be raised. We who are alive at that time (and Paul is not making any claim that he would be in that category—the 'we' simply means 'we Christians') will be transformed. Together we shall be found in our resurrection bodies, citizens of God's kingdom of heaven, not because of our own righteousness but because of what our Saviour has done for us.

And what of the rest? What of all those who have never even heard of God's mercy in Jesus Christ? What of all those who lived before he did? What of those who have sincerely followed other paths which they believed would bring them to God? The answer is found elsewhere in Paul's writing, perhaps most clearly in Romans 2:12–16. It is part of Paul's 'gospel' that the world will be judged by Jesus, which means that the One who judges is also the One who saves. No one could hope for a more understanding, compassionate and merciful Judge before whom to stand. And no one, we must believe, will leave that final assize feeling that they have been treated unjustly.

It is quite impossible for mortal men and women even to begin to imagine what life in the kingdom of heaven will be like, any more than a baby in the womb could imagine what life in the outside world is like. We have to take it on trust. But at least we know that the One who made this life so full of joy, surprise and splendour will be unlikely not to have saved a few joyful surprises for the next one.

37

Changed!

The trumpet shall sound, and the dead shall be raised incorruptible, and we shall be changed. For this corruptible must put on incorruption, and this mortal must put on immortality. Then shall be brought to pass the saying that is written, Death is swallowed up in victory. O death, where is thy sting? O grave, where is thy victory? The sting of death is sin; and the strength of sin is the law.

1 Corinthians 15:52–56

Everything changes at death, but when 'change' becomes 'transformation' the victory of God over death is complete.

This is St Paul's great hymn of victory over the grave. When we remember that it was written to Christians who had never expected to die, but to be carried off to heaven with the returning Saviour, it is all the more powerful. Suddenly, they are seeing their friends and relatives falling ill and dying. They are carrying their bodies to the tombs, wrapping them and burying them, for all the world as though Jesus had never risen from the dead and things were exactly as they'd always been. And they knew that within a day or two the process of decay would start to set in, and very soon their mortal bodies would begin to decompose. Was this the glorious 'new life in Christ' which the apostle had promised them?

Yes, it is, counters Paul. Though some Christians will be alive when Christ returns, some (little did he know how many!) would have died before it happens. That makes no difference to God's master plan. All along his purpose was that the mortal should become immortal, the corruptible should become incorruptible. From the start God had worked not for the preservation of human life, but its transformation.

It is, as we have seen, a serious misunderstanding of the Christian case to think of resurrection as something that brings our old bodies back to life. Medieval pictures and carvings may show dead bodies rising up through tombs and overturning grave-stones, but that is not what the Bible teaches. Our present, flesh and blood bodies cease to exist, either by the process of decay or through fire or even explosion. But God gives 'us', and by that I mean our self-aware human personalities, new bodies, perfectly fitted for life with him in eternity. 'Flesh and blood cannot inherit the kingdom of God', says Paul—so God gives us a body that can.

The resurrection body is both incorruptible—not subject to decay—and immortal, not subject to death. Unlike the body of Lazarus, which was raised from the dead but later died again, our new bodies are no longer subject to the physical processes of earth. Death no longer has dominion over them (see Romans 6:9).

Interestingly, in the same passage from Romans, St Paul also says that 'sin will have no dominion over you' (6:14)—drawing the same parallel as he does here. 'The sting of death is sin.' The point may seem an academic one, but in fact it is central to the Christian understanding of death. It was sin that brought about death (see Genesis 2:17 and 1 Corinthians 15:22), not, I think, in a physical sense but in a spiritual one. One could argue that the process of constant death and renewal which lies behind the whole working of nature seems to be part of God's creation. Leaves fall in autumn, flowers fade and die, animals and people reach the end of their lives, to be replaced by their off-spring. It was, however, God's purpose that death should bring us closer to him, as St Paul claims in one of his letters (Philippians 1:23). But sin spoiled things. It meant that far from bringing us closer to God, death created a final separation from him. There can be no sin in the presence of God. The two are totally incompatible. It is sin, in other words, that puts the 'sting' in death, changing it from nature's way of bringing us into the presence of God into separation from all that is true, beautiful and good.

And the 'sting' of sin is 'the law'. We can only sin if we do so wilfully. Whatever one of the prayers of Confession in the new Anglican services may have said, we can't sin 'by ignorance', because you cannot disobey a command that you do not know exists. (Happily, the phrase was changed to 'by negligence' in the final revision, a quite different thing!). So in one sense, the law of God, which is good, creates sin, which is evil. It is knowing what is wrong, and still doing it, that constitutes sin.

So the fearful combination of the good and holy Law of God, and my disobedience and wilfulness, creates sin. And sin causes spiritual death. But, as Handel is about to remind us, that is not the end of the story.

When a caterpillar is transformed into a butterfly, its life continues, but in a totally new and hitherto unimaginable environment. One day, we shall be freed from the confines of an earthly body, and experience the light, joy and freedom of life with God.

38

The final victory

But thanks be to God, who giveth us the victory through our Lord Jesus Christ.

1 Corinthians 15:57

If God be for us, who can be against us? Who shall lay any thing to the charge of God's elect? It is God that justifieth. Who is he that condemneth? It is Christ that died, yea rather, that is risen again, who is at the right hand of God, who makes intercession for us.

Romans 8:31, 33–34

If God himself has justified us, we need fear no accusations. If Christ has died for our sins, then there are no sins left to be dealt with. In both cases, the record is clean.

We are almost at the end of the story of redemption through the Messiah. The battle has been won. The enemy has been defeated. What remains is to tell the followers of the victory and encourage them to share in its benefits.

God gives us the victory. The present tense is important. It is not only that God won a mighty battle with evil in the life, death and resurrection of his Son, and that that battle is now over. It is also true that the fruits of that one, titanic conquest are still being worked out in the lives of Christians. We share in that victory now, day by day, as we see God moving on our behalf against the giants of fear, doubt, guilt and failure. Christians are not meant to be defeated people who are somehow miraculously rescued at the last minute! Every day we should be drawing on the power and inspiration of Christ's once-for-all victory on the cross.

It is through 'our Lord Jesus Christ' that we can have the victory. The (quite rare) use of his full title gives a distinct authority to this shout of thanks. He is the 'Lord', the Master; but he is our Lord and Master, too. He is 'Jesus', the Saviour, the one who would 'save his people from their sins'. He is 'Christ', which is the Greek form of 'Messiah'—he came in fulfilment of a long purpose of God, his anointed representative to our fallen race.

It is through his Son that God 'gives' us the victory. We don't earn it, or fight for it, or pay anything for it. The price has been paid, the battle has been fought. All that remains for us to do is to accept the victory he has won on our behalf.

That thought leads to another song of triumph, still in St Paul's words but now from the letter to the Romans. But this time it is a song not so much of Christ's victory, but of the people he calls 'the elect'. They are in an unassailable position. No one can lay any accusation against them because they have been 'justified' by God. No one can condemn them of any sin, not because they are especially 'good', but because 'Christ Jesus has died'—for their sins, that is. Not only that, but Christ is at the Father's right hand—the place of special honour and privilege—'interceding' for them, representing their cause. No wonder they can feel confident! Anyone would welcome being in a situation where no accusation could stand against them, they could not be condemned, and the most powerful figure in the universe was arguing their cause.

St Paul's case is that that is the position of all those who are 'in Christ'. The term 'elect' may seem strange to modern ears. Indeed, it may smack of a narrow and fanatical religion, of the kind where 'we' are 'in' and everybody else is definitely 'out'.

But it need have no such connotations. 'Elect' simply means 'chosen'. God chose Israel as the people through whom he would eventually reveal his purposes for the whole world. They were his 'elect' people of the old covenant. Now he has 'chosen' a new people, those who have gathered to his Messiah, in line with the unfolding of his purpose in the new covenant. But they have not been arbitrarily picked! 'Selection' is open to anyone! 'Everyone who calls on the name of the Lord shall be saved', says Paul in this same letter (Romans 10:13). God has no favourites, as St Peter has to learn (Acts 10:34). The offer of eternal life in Jesus is available to all, on the same basis for everybody: faith in the Son of God.

That, we can now see, was the whole object of the exercise. That was why God's Messiah came. That is the magnificent purpose of God revealed through his risen and ascended Son.

A REFLECTION

The confidence which the Christian is meant to have is not in his or her own righteousness, but in the grace and love of God and the death and resurrection of Jesus. Once we have grasped that, we shall be very unlikely to take it for granted, or presume on the grace of God.

THE TRIUMPH OF
THE MESSIAH

The last section of *Messiah* is no other than a song of triumph, celebrating the final victory of the 'Lamb of God' over sin and evil. Its setting is heaven, in the splendid imagery of Revelation. The vision is of a Lamb 'looking as if it had been slain'—we might say 'with the marks of slaughter on it'. He is deemed able to open the mysterious scroll of God's purpose, sealed with seven seals. As he does so, a great scene of worship erupts. Golden bowls of incense—'the prayers of the saints'—waft into the air. Harps take up their music. And the 'living creatures' and the twenty-four 'elders' begin to sing a new song, the song of the triumph of the Lamb, by the shedding of whose blood a people has been 'purchased' for God from every tribe and language and nation.

Before this vision, the only response is adoration. The enemy has been vanquished. Mankind has been liberated from the long enslavement of sin. At last, the Messiah's work may be celebrated.

39

The blood of the Lamb

Worthy is the Lamb that was slain, and hath redeemed us to God by his blood, to receive power, and riches, and wisdom, and strength, and honour, and glory, and blessing. Blessing, and honour, glory and power, be unto him that sitteth upon the throne, and unto the Lamb for ever and ever.

Revelation 5:12–13

The most striking thing about heaven is that right at its heart is the perfect picture of undeserved suffering: the wounded hands and feet of the Son of God.

Back in the 1970s I remember broadcasting a remarkable interview on Radio 4. Edmund Wilbourne was a Captain in the Church Army who had been certified dead in a Manchester hospital, but 'came back to life' in the mortuary two hours later. During the intervening time he had undergone a 'near-death experience' of quite extraordinary clarity, which he described on the programme. In the course of this experience he met Jesus Christ, recognizing him by the wounds of the nails in his hands and feet. As he thought ruefully at the time, they were 'the only man-made things in heaven'.

It is that strange paradox that lies at the heart of these visionary words from Revelation. They focus on 'the Lamb'—'the Lamb that was slain'. It is he who is worthy to receive riches and power and glory—strange honours for a slaughtered animal. But it is precisely because the Lamb had been 'slain' that these honours are now his.

The 'Lamb', of course, is Jesus Christ. As we have already seen in *Messiah*, he is 'the Lamb of God that taketh away the sin of the world'. While that imagery may seem alien to modern minds, biblical culture was steeped in it, and if we ourselves are truly to 'honour the Lamb' then we probably need to try to get inside the principle that lies behind it.

From the earliest days of the history of the Hebrew people—right back to God's first covenant with Abraham—the offering of a lamb or a goat as a sacrifice was a mark of a price paid. Indeed, in the dawn of the biblical story, the cause of the dispute between

Cain and Abel was the nature of the sacrifices they offered to God. Cain offered 'the fruits of the soil' while Abel offered animal sacrifices. 'The Lord had regard for Abel and his offering' (Genesis 4:4). In some way, it was seen as fitting that humans should give back to God his most precious gift, which is life itself. 'The life of the flesh is in the blood', says Leviticus (17:11). Human sacrifice was not unknown in the heathen nations around them, but Israel learnt a different way—the death of innocent animals and birds, by which sin was forgiven and an acceptable living sacrifice made to God. The fact that most modern people find the whole process revolting cannot alter the fact that sacrifice has always been an element in religious worship, as though it meets some deep instinctive human need to make atonement and to offer something of unique value to God, that is, life itself.

The coming of Jesus Christ put to an end the whole necessity for animal sacrifices. As the letter to the Hebrews puts it, 'It is impossible for the blood of bulls and goats to take away sins' (10:4). But now the true Lamb was to be offered, as one sacrifice for sins for ever, voluntarily made and to be received by faith. 'Every priest stands day after day at his service, offering again and again the same sacrifices that can never take away sins. But when Christ had offered for all time a single sacrifice for sins, "he sat down at the right hand of God"' (Hebrews 10:11–12).

That is why Jesus is called the 'Lamb of God'. That is how he can be said to 'take away the sins of the world'. And that is why, in John's vision of the glory of heaven, universal worship is offered to 'the Lamb that was slain'.

When Jesus appeared to his disciples in the upper room on the evening of the first Easter Day, he 'showed them his hands and his side' (John 20:20)—the wounds of his death on the cross. John records, 'Then were the disciples glad...' It was not the thought that he had suffered that made them happy, but the confirmation of two things: the one who stood before them truly was Jesus, and their sins were truly forgiven. As St Peter put it in his first letter (echoing the prophecy of Isaiah long ago), 'By his wounds you have been healed' (2:24). They were the visible proof of the reality of Christ's sacrifice. In that sense, they were wounds to be honoured: 'Worthy is the Lamb that was slain and hath redeemed us to God by his blood, to receive power and riches and wisdom and strength and honour and glory and blessing'.

A man was rescued by his mother from a blazing bedroom when he was a baby. In doing so, she was dreadfully burned and her face was permanently scarred. Others who meet her would say that her face was disfigured, but he simply says, 'To me, those scars are beautiful, because they say how much my mother loved me.' When we honour the Lamb that was slain we honour his wounds, because, as the hymn says, they are 'the marks of love'.

And they are the proof of God's eternal love for his creatures. The death of Jesus for us was not the result of arbitrary human injustice, nor a secondary plan of salvation when all else had failed. 'The Lamb was slain from the creation of the world' (Revelation 13:8). In some mysterious way, our sin and rebellion were foreseen and God's purpose of love and salvation for his disobedient creatures was planned before the creation of the world.

That is why the story of God's Messiah is the story of eternity. That is why the coming of the Christ was the great theme of the Hebrew prophets and the most glorious refrain of the psalmists of Israel. That is why angels sang in the fields below Bethlehem, and visited a quiet olive grove outside Jerusalem to strengthen the Messiah as he faced death.. That is why there was a cross and an empty tomb. That is why the coming of the Messiah is, quite simply, the most important thing that ever happened, and what he did on earth the most glorious story ever told.

A REFLECTION

In the light of the whole story of Messiah, can we see the coming of Jesus as part of the great purpose of God for the human race? And can we see his wounds as instruments of healing, for us, and for the suffering nations of the earth?

40

The amen principle

Amen.

Revelation 5:14

How else could *Messiah* end than with the response of the people to the words they have heard?

Messiah ends with a very long and elaborate 'Amen', begun by the basses, picked up by the tenors and then the altos, and finally involving the whole chorus in a splendid hymn of triumphant praise. We are all used to 'amen' as the last word of a prayer or a hymn, sometimes almost as a kind of reflex action, but here Handel gives the single word enormous weight and importance.

It is very appropriate that he should. For the 'Amen Chorus' is not simply a tidy way to round off the whole work. It is an invitation to the hearer to respond to its message.

'Amen' is a Hebrew word, transliterated into Greek by the New Testament writers and taken over into every language in which Christian worship is offered. I recall standing in a sunlit street in Baden Baden, in Germany, listening to a group of Russian monks chanting their prayers and hymns. It occurred to me that the only word of what they sang which I could recognize and understand was 'Amen'—pronounced, in their case, as 'Ameen'. Yet one was drawn to share in some way in their prayer and praise, and 'amen' was a very good means of expressing that solidarity.

'Amen' means, literally, 'truth'. In saying 'amen' to a prayer, we are accepting it as 'truth'... not just abstract truth, truth to be believed, but truth for us. 'Amen' says, in effect, 'me too'. It involves me in the worship or prayer of another person, and makes it mine. It also has an active sense—'may this be true', 'may this come to pass', 'so be it'. To say 'amen', therefore, is to do much more than simply concur. It is to commit oneself to the truth that is being sung or celebrated or the hope that is being turned into prayer.

So it is here. We have heard the worship of heaven, the great echoing song of 'ten thousand times ten thousand angels' encircling the throne of God. They have called us to honour the Lamb who was slain. We have also heard the song of 'every creature in heaven and on earth', offering blessing and honour and glory and power' to 'Him that sitteth upon the throne and unto the Lamb'. Now we join with the 'four living creatures' and the 'elders' in saying 'Amen', 'so be it'; and with them we 'fall down and worship' (see Revelation 5:12–14).

In his rather angry letter to the Galatians, St Paul has a wonderful parenthesis to his main argument, in which he describes his own life as a Christian. 'I have been crucified with Christ', he says. 'And it is no longer I who live, but it is Christ who lives in me. And the life I now live in the flesh I live by faith in the Son of God, who loved me and gave himself for me' (Galatians 2:20–21). Usually Paul speaks of Christ dying for us, or for 'the Church', or for 'the sins of the world'. But here, uniquely, and (by the structure of his sentence) with great emphasis, he says, 'Christ loved me, and gave himself for me'.

That is the 'Amen' principle! It's the recognition that a universal truth has been personally appropriated. The Lamb who was slain is on the throne of heaven, true. But he was the Lamb slain for me, and my 'Amen' makes that wonderful truth mine. No wonder Handel has us singing 'Amen' over and over again—no less than 43 times, by my reckoning! The Lamb who was slain is worthy of praise… God who loved us and sent his Messiah is to receive praise and glory and power for ever and ever. Yes, it is true—and it is my truth!

A REFLECTION

At the end of the whole story of God's purposes for us through his Messiah, it seems appropriate to pause and reflect on its message. We began by thinking how monumental a work Handel and Jennens had embarked on—nothing less than the epic story of the dealings of God with the human race. As the vast panorama of God's purpose stretched out before them they must have felt that they had taken on more than any human could possibly comprehend. Yet at the end, as we stand with them before the sheer magnificence of God's love for us in Christ, we can perhaps see with fresh eyes the grace and the glory that inspired this composition. It is not a story simply to read, or listen to, or enjoy. It is a story that brings us to our knees in adoration. When we have reached that point, then with earthly and angelic choirs we too can add our own 'Amen'. So be it.

NOTES FOR
GROUP STUDY

If you are using this book with a group, you might find these suggestions for discussion useful. They are based on the different sections of the book.

Session 1: Promise and warning

There is obviously some conflict between those who feel that God welcomes us 'as we are', and those who feel that our approach to him should be reverent and preceded by preparation and repentance. This is reflected in people's different approaches to worship, for instance. The group might like to share their own feelings about this. How do the group respond to Isaiah's call (echoed by John the Baptist) that we should prepare ourselves for the coming of God into our lives by repentance and 'amendment of life'? Does this create an unnecessary 'hurdle' in the journey of faith? How do we balance for ourselves the elements of 'fear' (or awe) and of confident love in our approach to God?

Session 2: The birth of the Messiah

What difference does the incarnation (the coming of God's Son as a human being) make to our understanding of God and our own faith? If Jesus of Nazareth was truly the Son of God, rather than simply a great prophet or teacher, what effect does that have on our response to what he said and did? Does it make a great deal of difference to believe that he was born of a virgin? And in what way could his coming be seen as making 'peace on earth' possible?

Session 3: The life of the Messiah

Jesus came with a message—'The kingdom of God'. In this section of *Messiah* the oratorio emphasizes the personal aspects of the kingdom—healing, forgiveness, personal freedom, strength and comfort. Members of the group may wish to share their own experiences of these blessings. But it also speaks of a Messiah who will bring 'righteousness and peace'. This raises an important question: How do we relate individual blessing and healing to the needs of our community as a whole? How does the 'kingdom of God' bring together individual blessing and blessing for the whole world?

Session 4: **The suffering Messiah**

Members of the group might be prepared to share personal experiences of being 'abandoned' by others, or of being ridiculed at some point in their lives. It may help to start from our own experience of such things, and our recollected *reaction* to them—anger, depression, indignation, desire for revenge... or sheer, abject disintegration. We can then compare our own reactions to abandonment and scorn with those of Jesus. How significant for us is it that he went through these experiences in the course of his death 'for the sins of the world'?

When you have done that, you might like to think as a group how you see the whole idea of 'atonement'—how what Jesus did 2,000 years ago can bring about the forgiveness of our sins today.

Session 5: **The risen Messiah**

What do you think are the main difficulties modern people have with the whole idea of the resurrection of Jesus? And—as we are called to share this 'good news' with others—how would we set about answering them? *Messiah* clearly sees the resurrection as a great victory, with eternal consequences. How can that aspect of the 'good news' be reflected in a world where it doesn't *look* as though good has triumphed over evil?

Session 6: **King of kings**

Here we have brought together the sections headed 'The Messiah king', 'Life through the Messiah' and 'The triumph of the Messiah', as they all deal with the *consequences* of the victory of Christ effected in his resurrection and celebrated in his ascension.

The consequences, according to the New Testament, are that 'eternal life' becomes a possibility for everyone who puts their faith in Jesus. How do we understand that idea? *Messiah*—following St Paul—links Christ's resurrection to ours, but what does that mean in practice? Do we think of a bodily resurrection (like Christ's)—but with what kind of body? You might like to look, as a group, at the passage in 1 Corinthians on which *Messiah* draws very heavily (15:35–57).

These suggestions are simply that—suggestions! The 'Reflections' at the end of each chapter may also provide material for discussion, or for a group meditation.

If you have enjoyed reading *Forty Days with the Messiah*, you may wish to know that David Winter is a regular contributor to *New Daylight*, a regular series of daily Bible reading notes, published by The Bible Reading Fellowship three times a year (in January, May and September). *New Daylight* contains printed Bible passages, brief comments and prayers and is also available in a large print version.

Copies of *New Daylight* may be obtained from your local Christian bookshop or by subscription direct from BRF.

A free sample copy of *New Daylight* may be obtained by sending an A5 SAE with 36p stamp marked '*New Daylight*' to BRF.

For more information about the full range of BRF publications, write to: The Bible Reading Fellowship, Peter's Way, Sandy Lane West, Oxford OX4 5HG. Tel. 01865 748227. Fax 01865 773150